*<u>The Kiss In Slaughterhouse 6</u> *

Sunny Jetsun

<u>The Kiss In Slaughterhouse 6</u> *

<u>Other Books Published by Sunny Jetsun</u>

'Driving My Scooter Through The Asteroid Field
Coming Down Over Venus ~ "Hallo Baba"

**'Light love Angels from Heaven. New Generation,
Inspiration, Revolution, Revelation ~
All the Colours of Cosmic Rainbows'**

'Green Eve * Don't lose the Light Vortex *
My brain's gone on holiday ~ free flowing feelings'

**'Surfing or Suffering together * Sense Consciousness
fields of a body with streams and stars of hearts'**

'When You're happy you got wings on your back ~
Reposez vos oreilles a Goa; We're only one kiss away"'

'PSYCHIC PSYCHEDELIC'

'Streaming Lemon Topaz Sunbeams'

'Invasion of Beauty *FLASH * The Love Mudras'

'Patchouli Showers ~ Tantric Temples'

'It's Just a Story We Are All The Sun, Sweet Surrender'

Anthology #1 ~ 'Enjoy The Revolution'

Anthology # 2 ~ 'Love & Freedom ~ Welcome'

'He Lives In A Parallel Universe'

'Queen of Space King of Flower Power dripping Rainbows'

'All Love Frequency ~ In Zero Space'

*Peace Goddess*Spirit of the Field*The Intimacy Sutras*

'Heavenly Bodies ~ Celestial Alignments*
Feeling ~ Energy that Is LOVE in Itself'

**'I've been to Venus & back*These Are Real Feelings*
Let the Universe Guide Your Heart*through Space'**

One word can cast a Magical spell, grammar going right under the radar, the subliminal tongue. Underestimating the Power of the word, of language creating your unique perception ~ Allowing it to manifest through your own filters acting in the brain's time*space chemistry. Who is manufacturing this, our consent, this mass conditioning, lies, identity to judge others, judging Oneself? Brainwashing Forms an 'online encyclopedia' of predetermined reactions and responses. 'In the beginning was the word' the 'logos' having an Immediate effect on y/our/mass consciousness, on our world and Planet*Cosmos!

*

'A narcissistic personality disorder causes problems in many areas of life such as relationships, work, financial affairs school You may be generally unhappy and disappointed when you're not given the special favours or admiration you believe you deserve. Others may not enjoy being by you, you may find your relationships unfulfilling.' (Wikipedia)

*

Rumi: 'In the mirror of infinite consciousness reflections are seen which constitute the appearance of the world'

*

Sunny Jetsun Online at:
Website: www.sunnyjetsun.com
Facebook: www.facebook.com/sunnyjetsun
Smashwords:www.smashwords.com/profile/view/sunnyjetsun
Amazon: www.amazon.com/author/sunnyjetsun

She Sucked You All In
When the curtain finally drops!
There is no law and no order.
A M A Z I N G * N A T U R E
With aspirations for a better System.
Put it all out on the table
Let your children work it out ~
Our future Ideal Vision.
Why the f... do you go to work every day?
Anyway, no time to think about it!

*

Shakti has left the room
Don't know who you really are....
Can't do it for you, only doing it for yourself.
People affected by your light, underlying Awareness.
The Total Conditioning of Fear & Desire.
Wanting it all, it's not true only an Illusion.
LOVE you have to find it in You.
Real because it's not dependent on others.
Blooming like a beautiful flower

*

Core to everything
They have a right to be here in nature.
Your compassion for other people ~
is good for the other Spirit.
Nature doesn't kill bacteria
It lives with it

They can make Life*Enjoy the Illusion
They can give you drama too ~ They give you everything!
Belief in 72 virgins waiting in Paradise, all hallucinations,
Non-existing fantasy when you've a beautiful, devoted wife!
If there was an ultimate secret knowledge what would it be?
Only Soul mate is God, only one who can see you as a Soul.
"It's all talks" Enjoy Loving yourself ~ that moment Satguru.
If you believe in God, you believe in humans too ~
It's your energy not hers; Her energy ignites the flame!
Play with your romantic nature but don't get trapped ~
Shakti women*Angels from Heaven, vampires from Hell.
Magic starting to glow in between her wet, moist thighs.
Kamashakti "If you can conquer your sexual desires ~
sitting on your Tiger mat, no woman can disturb you!"
Shiva controls his passion ~ Shakti is nature....
'Being his servant means you are the Queen
of the Universe'

*

LOVE YOURSELF
According to our wishes, be good, be thankful
Sorry no production of a Love movie today. No Choices…
Convert or die the Church is your mother, King is your father!
"I can control you through my God because now you accepted
him as your God." ~ Doing what you're told, join in our gang.

*

…Ai * Wei
..Wu * Wei

No Antidote

Microdot bonbons, white lightning sweets ~
Purple haze, California Sunshine sunbathing.
Double dipped "I'm not here to tax my brain"
"If they put the money into something good
not shit, the world would be a better place"
'Your perception is being steamrollered'
Talking people into their own fields ~
She was full of life, looked really happy
High Energy

*

Program Globally Available Chip

"If that is your first dick and the only dick
you know you won't want another dick!"
"A girl with early sexual experience
will never be satisfied." Programming...
Sexual looking tribal chicks, full devotion.
"When you get your cake and you
want to keep the cake, why not?"
Destroying embedded Programming
'Hypocrisy part of human nature.com'
'She's fucked it off, it doesn't work!'
How was your life as a child dear?
'Now is the Future*Past doesn't exist!'
'Time is a healer so they say ~ saw Angels
chakras opening*unconditional Love

Klitty*Hoodie
It's all in the Mix ~
It's Not Psychedelic
there are No Hippies!
Party crowd does all the drugs.
Flipped out she's a Psycho
tied him to the water bed,
wanted to cut his dick off!
"I own it, got a plot of Mars"
Start with let the chemistry
do what will happen
Smile say 'Hallo', Anything
can happen & pass the Joint!
'If you don't it won't'

*

Reward or Punishment
Parameters of 'Our Identity' State.
Human beings appreciating the Grand
Illusory State of Maya, until they step out.
Compassion transmuting ~ Mind >'Mine-Form'
No Personal attachment means I got nothing to Fear.
'No personal Image so you got No thing to defend....
Know you are Identifying with an Illusion ~ Change your Mind-set.
All you are doing is re/acting out your conditioning, programming.
It shouldn't need the 'losing it' or 'finding it' swinging dual pendulum.
Making assumptions and judgments ~ not feeling Life's Presence

Truman*Mesmerised

'Think in a certain way to make you positive, happy'
Obeying the Rules of a hard Corporate takeover!
Once you see the curtain drop you see it all.
The Empress without her Victoria's secrets
Spending all that energy to hide it more.
86 vaccinations delivered to your baby
'Never let a thought take Control!'
Sold the Police, making a Profit!
It's all out there on Mercury
You're not being depressed

*

Heartfelt Relationship

You broke my balls, heart & mind but not my Spirit
This is a Meditation alternative ~ Centering point.
Been in bleak, black places in my head
Stand up for your rights, challenge the System.
Believing in the beautiful Magic.
How you are looking at things ~
Good drugs, put it out on the street Socrates!
Giving it out and gratitude for getting it back.
I don't need any license, validation, Certificate.
Love, love different types, your love is about you,
Loving me for who I am.

<u>FREE*WHEELING*SUN</u>
Sublimely beautiful, marvelous Krishna
Not Exclusive, All Inclusive, infinite.
No Separation for Maya to appear
No Schizophrenia of Mind projections.
Letting Ego's illusions go in the flow ~
What is this emotion? Being here now
The only way to come out of a black hole is
by letting the Universe take over Completely.
Surrendering to the Loving Kindness
'Life's a super radiant biche'
*

<u>On the Consequences of our actions</u>
*Depends on recognising*what's the effects?*
Maybe Other people in that relationship/
situation are left with their own overwhelming
consequences when you've made a 'catastrophic'
'life changing' choice/I had No other choice!"
Back to the human obsess attachment syndrome!
There are innumerable examples.. just try not
to be Ignorant but be kind:) and who can say?*
'You may have to be cruel to be kind, she said!'
How about 'do unto others as you will
have done unto you' and what's
Universal synchronicity gotta do with it?

Not Knowing About It
Psychedelic Trance*Positive Intention.
"When's the Crash coming?"
Came as a Force for Good ~
Not the debt based illusion model.
Who's got all the Gold?
Finland asked for theirs returned
from the Bank of the Global Illuminati
without success as its all **f**.... disappeared.
I'm sure the Chancellor does what he's told mate.
Sold all the Treasury's bling, bling for a fucking pittance!
*

Routers' Stress Techniques
Compromised all the Trust not by any accident!
Their Master plan all the time Mr & Mrs Innocent.
Monitoring millions of people, under what law?
Ownership of You & Your Privacy do you agree?
Offensive Cyber Operations, for the whistleblower
regretted he never exposed their nastiness earlier.
"I burned my life to the ground."Against Surveillance
A marked man, 'Extraordinary Rendition' call it what
You will, Trauma or drama, He now feels truly blessed.
All Crimes against humanity from Inside Palatial walls.
Left a golden asset on their doorstep... 'Quid pro Quo'
"Tu vas dormir avec ton Robot?"

~ Smiling eyes ~
Falling crystal snowflakes everywhere.
A mystical yogini with the golden hair
Peace Love and Happiness to you
I've fallen in Love with a Gazelle.

*

Weeping Woman
'Without Money we'd all be Rich'
Even the dogs here aren't wagging their tales anymore!
'Assault on women with intent to outrage her modesty'
A little boy found lying dead on a beach with his mum.
The sweet sandalwood smell of burning life ~
He was not at all generous in Love
Just send him a stick of dynamite!

*

'For Crimes Against God'
"These are all your whores not other people's whores!"
The worst 'rumour-mongers' will be sentenced to death,
while lesser offenders of the new policy will be disciplined
with flogging, amputation, imprisonment, travel bans,
house arrest, fines and social media bans.

*

Desolation Verified
"We WON!" ~The last Species left on the Planet!
Doubling levels of Artificial Intelligence paradigms
while halving the Living population of the World!
Drilled a hole to let the sand out ~
Stopping Fucking About!

These were leaders and there were many many many more
some obvious ones are missing. Going through the Nobel
Peace Prize list you will find a few for eg. Aung San Suu Kyi
who continued her struggle in solitude just like many
whistleblowers out there or stuck inside a dark cell!
A Revolutionary is what exactly? Someone who fights
for the truth Against Injustice and very often sacrifices their
life and the lives of their loved ones! The courage to be a
'Revolutionary' is also with the Unknown one who died alone
often tortured. Let's not turn this into a Pop Culture Quiz with
the Prize of a Free T shirt. Trotsky some say was a New York
banker sent by the Illuminati to bankroll, pull the strings for what
was their own Political/Economic agenda! Who is a Pure, true
Revolutionary? Jesus definitely, Buddha is Revolution ~ &
all those who support, risk their lives for Peace Not Oppression!

*

"I Lied!"

'There I was the only white guy at the Star of Bethlehem ~
"Yeah he was an Extra-terrestrial*Objective-Mental illusion!"
We can transcend suffering apparently, it is said, or at least
it can be put up with and fully realized. It's not a bad quest
if you can keep up a smile until you can bear it no more
then you can surrender and continue in peace.
Radiating Inner Awareness

Realisation

You were so in Love that you thought it would be forever ~
*It was a **deep Shock** when you found out that it wasn't!*
Does she realise now that she's lost the most wonderful
thing in her life or she accepts it as just another part ~
of the journey? Making it through the Venus Universe.

*

The Last Lagoon

(Ref. MARIKO MORI: Creative Artist.)
Art Engaging All the Senses
Extending our Vocabulary & Mind...
'AI.' *AFFECTIONATE*INTIMACY*
'AUTOMATICISM*INHUMANISM'
Narcissistic*Nihilistic ~ Unholistic
Losing our feelings for each other.
****MOTHER * EARTH****
SHE'S A*FULL* FLOWER *
POWER *LOVE*ENERGY

All of US

Peace * light * feelings
Our destiny here * now ~ be a hero.
Be strong & courageous*AS You Are ~
Holding, channeling Inspirational Power
Embracing Universal Spirit ~ flowing
with Love in your heart

10

Once I read a 'Dictionary of Battles' which showed
that historically humans in parts of the world have
been murdering, raping, pillaging and massacring other
human beings (Who as the enemy either deserved it
or not or for just being in the way or they had some
hidden treasure!) since the beginning, which in this
book went back to Egyptian pharaohs. Even the holy
'Bhagavad Gita' is basically about winning a war for the
good old reasons of family, feud, revenge over a woman,
an insult, cheating over property, a crime whatever you like
that eventually pisses you off! Now this violence seems to
be a part of human nature and either you win or lose through
spirituality, where you realise it's all material illusion so it doesn't
matter if you get a spear in your head or you get tooled up with
the biggest battle axe or canon or horse or hero or Zeus or Arjuna
to help you. Or you sacrifice a few slaves to God or blow up a school
bus or drop a Patriot missile on a wedding party or hospital by mistake!
It's a f.....g collateral mess for those who happen to be 'Target de jour!'
And for what? We are obviously still poor barbarians or worse and it is
throughout the culture/system/indoctrination/Ideology as in '1984'
At least by realising that our enemy could be from the next village and
to treat everyone kindly, humanely, then we all have a better chance to
HAVE A HAPPY DAY***:)

*

Seeing the Truth
In the Realm of the Ego State ~
The Real Knowing Is 'Not Knowing it'
Thinking puts an Illusion in the Space.

Psyche*Pachimama*Signal

"Not much I can do about it" "just be yourself"
That Green Screen again projecting our Form of reality!
It's what you perceive, transmit, receive of Gaia frequency
"Do you believe in miracles, in Paranirvana vibrations?"
Recognising that we are ALL ultimately ~
MULTI*DIMENSIONALLY FREE BEINGS
On different planes of realisation ~ existence.
Killed them all, couldn't look him in the face again!
Still ~ seems like a long way to go to find an Angel.
Already infiltrated me with a beautiful Russian bride.
Genuinely really happy people ~ like life's a holiday.

*

Oxytocin Vapours

Coke 'S/he really Loves it' .. Brainwashing Coda!
It ain't the perfect thing! And ask about Codex
Alimentarius! "I like Mission Impossible don't you?"
"I like the Muppets!"
Why beat yourself up? Trusting in your Divine nature.
Sufi's always new and fresh as soon as you let go ~
"If you can Love yourself give yourself a kiss!"

*

Snowden

'An International defender of human rights, civil liberties
and privacy.' Made a genuine application for Asylum in 21
countries and was refused. Told to surrender himself and he
wouldn't be tortured! US Appeal court vindicated his actions…

Stella Winds

How would you like a lifetime in solitary confinement
without trial? Ask Mordecai Vanunu or Miss Manning.
At the time I thought he was edgy, tense and paranoid.
Cruel inhumane treatment, how about a Death Penalty?
'That's the last time we'll see him interview.'
Under the Pretext of the preventing of Terrorism.
Who is morally right to fight for law and constitution?
Exposing criminality and Secret Government Gestapos!
Remember Extraordinary rendition & Stress techniques!
Forgotten Water-boarding not now in the Media spotlight!
"He'd gone public, gone to the Guardian"
"He was going to be smashed!" Sacrificed!
That's tough to organise 'Operation Asylum'
Ask Wiki leaks; He's charged with Espionage!
A White House task Force on his tail.
"It's his decision it's his life!"
"We needed to move"

*

Consorting

Real men treat their women between being
a Spirit Goddess and a Queen because
you need a Woman by your side as an Equal ~
sharing in the light not like a young inexperienced needy Princess.
The above is true when the woman recognises her man as a King.
The Queen Ultimately doesn't need the understanding of a man
as she Knows that whatever happens she is a Queen
and she can also Give the gift of listening to his feelings
and both know the Magic and reflect its beauty
for each other and the rest of nature*:)

<u>On the record price paid for a Picasso, $179 million</u>
Does anyone prefer the Picasso that was sold last week for a
record price $179 million? Also there was the highest price paid
for a 20 carat blood red ruby and a sculpture by Giacometti.
At least it was bought at auction in a 'free market' for billionaires.
However it does seem clear that objects are worth a lot more
than Life itself, UNFORTUNATELY*and God kicked Adam
& Eve out of Paradise for eating an apple * and still he has
never forgiven them and nothing much has changed since
the beginning of time! Very sad but don't we agree that Life
is intrinsically more amazing than these seeming perversions!
And Adam is still loving Eve somewhere and Rothko (see Rothko/
Picasso in 'The Power of Art' by Simon Schama, BBC) had a great
creative soul as did Picasso and the price of Art shouldn't distract us
from our human brilliance in an apathetic, greedy, Ego Capitalist world.

*

To be honest I wouldn't buy it even if I had the money to 'Invest.' If
Picasso's name wasn't on it I wouldn't pay $179. However the same
rational could be applied to many other things eg. football players' wages,
but again I never go to a football match. It's not my money that is being
spent, then the question is where did that money originally come from?
Basically it's all corruption until each person is able to have a basic living
with nourishment & security etc. That seems unrealistic only in the sense
that we would have to change the economic/psychological paradigms but
it is a basis for humanity and the Planet to survive in Peace. Is there any
example of this existing today? Some say Iceland but then there is always
the fear of Genghis Khan or any other tyrant turning up at your front door

*Still development of human consciousness would be a good
step forward BUT do the people in power want to risk losing
their Power? It's another contradiction that at least shows
the rest of us how things are working within their Matrix
and then it's up to us to 'Live the life we want to see in the
World'. Take a look at the insanity on the News today and
ask is this right?**:)*

*

Hypnotism we all know!
*Hiding from the light*Cosmic Spatial cowboy
"The main thing a girl wants is comfort"
"I should get some soft fluffy cushions"
'16,000 wives, each has their own Palace!'
All Lakshmi super magnetism manifestations ~
Shiva Lord of the material, Vishnu is the Spiritual.
Shiva meditating on Vishnu, his higher self.
Brahma's passion and creativity of Life.*

*

A song of 18 verses
*"Leave every religion just surrender your ego to Krishna"
Heaven and Hell is material not supreme consciousness.
The Super soul inside your soul ~ can't see him,
he knows, he's Vishnu directly sharing energy.
The mightiest warriors aiming their lances at you!
Krishna enlightened him there on the battlefield.
All he needed to be liberated from the Kala yuga.
It's all Illusions, addictions of your holographic mind.
Invite Krishna into your heart ~ you can win the war
inside ~ outside with your own self and be in Heaven*

<u>Vienna Convention Waltzing Strudel</u>
'War is directly linked and manipulated
with the perception of territory & Nationalism.'
The visible power structures exposed showing
the true nature of a Puppet Europe.
The tide going out showing the power relations
between the US/EU's structures underneath ~
President Obama was awarded a Nobel Peace Prize
at the beginning of his M. I. Complex Empire tenure.'
"For his extraordinary efforts to strengthen international
diplomacy and cooperation between peoples." WTF!

*

<u>Empathy Giving Metta</u>
~ Your Smile Is the Sunshine ~
Your (work) Creativity is Inspirational
keeping it simple, natural, high and light.
Am I having a Magical Tantric Fantasy,
Imagining I'm an Energetic Love Healer?
'Selfish, greedy' what the fuck was that?
Reminiscing on an illusory, sparkling Jewel of an Ego!
At the Ganges on Mars ~ "he's one gig short of a terabyte."
"She looked very disappointed when I asked her for a kiss"
Everything is up for a fire Sale today even Love.
Lost all Sense of direction ~
Has a big charisma, lovely personality, sweet, fresh.
Being more Unconditional.

Inside the Temple
Sat forever in a non-stop streaming glorious golden light.
If you go to the Spiritual Universe You won't come back.
Desire fulfilling trees dancing with Krishna.
"If you Stop you'll get a rebirth!"
"One gram of DNA holds as much
Information as 600 billion CDs."

*

Not in My Name
"I know nothing it's all Mad!"
"It even got through my barrier of not giving a fuck.
Now it's What the fuck!!!"
Fining the homeless, bombing those other people!
It's really cold living on the street in winter.
No one wants to be crashing in a doorway
except for the wo/man who's lost all hope!
'No one can hurt me without my consent'
Ask Freedom Fighter, Mahatma Gandhi.

*

Eugenic Pharmacology
It's the first of many operations required.
And here is your bill with your box of pills.
And here is your narcissistic spectrum baby.
Vodka in the broken water ~ unstable moods.
Vaccines to make a child do this or that program.
Not naturally growing up.

Misrepresenting Machiavelli's Strategy

You gotta have faith in nature, regaining our Power.
Now Northern California is worse than F... North Korea!
Levels of Suppression, lies, propaganda, assassination.
Windows 101, Big bully brother, Spy ware in the kitchen.
"Who's talking about whom matey?"
"It's the end of the World granny!"
Sucking all the money out the system ~ And
using us all as Slaves ~ Divides & Conquers.
All the money on Earth at their own disposal.
Choice between this and that democratic twat!
Sit back and watch the virtual show unfold ~
Freedom or solitary, poverty, confusion, fear?
We're all being desensitised.

*

Making a Happy Decision

Drove Myself Crazy ~ Just how I was Thinking.
Looking at something in my mind
feeling the emotion and a smile.
Changing the way you look at it
Whether you like it or not!
'Once bitten twice shy' is the saying
Your Spirit will carry you ~
The world can be a bad place.
"I didn't make the world but it's up to me"
Embracing the Space with the things you like.
Adrenalin's good for you... Gotta get on it!

Still Traumatised, Fuck!
Butterflies in the world ~
"Flying spacemen not human
they have no compassion!"
My Lover denied my existence
like she never even knew me ~
He couldn't support the hypocrisy!
Hey man we're Universal children.

*

Korean Program So What!
Fans of silk, red dog meat, dried rat take yu pick!
Sentimental honey talkers taking your life away.
'Martial law, that's when people disappeared'
When they went to the Beauty Pageant in Chad!
You meet smart girls, she was reading the Koran.
Commentaries of hate not from the Persian poet.
"You have to overcome Self, becoming subject to self.
'God loves a Trier' ~ You have to die to self"
Imagination is insane in the future, all imagined illusions.
All sorts of apparent reality going on inside my head.
Just clear that, just accept it for what it is.
Attention itself is Vital ~ identifying a sound.
Purely responding to a direct need.
"I'm not religious ~ I believe in the Happy day"
They're kind and nice, they'll ignore you in Jerusalem.
You're offering me Freedom, putting me back in Bondage!
Following the path is a big obstacle ~ being of it not in it.
For the highest self, no preconditioning, being here now.
'You made me a King'

<u>Touchy Screen</u>
Artificial Intelligence ~
Rather have chillout music
"Wish I had that magic motivator to
hypnotise shaved pussycats to fuck!"
Unbelievable blowjobs! Fingering a tight
arse cunt. Stretching those velvet lips ~
Living his own blissful life in his harem.
"Give her that Cosmic cum let her taste it!"
Didn't matter if you were smoking a chillum
at the side of the road; To disconnect from the material!
What's Christian about bombing all those Arabs to dust?
Jesus wouldn't do that he would embrace them!
He showed you how to have a good vibe ~
and you didn't do it. So why come back?
Linking up the Planet to Love, they didn't...

*

<u>Why allow them to hurt you</u>?
Not making woman an emotional but a physical need.
"Inner happiness doesn't depend on a chick."
It's a beautiful delusion spun by Kamadev.
"Splitting up is a thankful experience darling!"
Understanding, ask what this life is teaching you.
Not being attached to pleasure with pain's irony.
Giving out Peace to the Universe ~
feeling in the moment ~ with you.

*

<u>Sunlit*Goa</u>
Higher consciousness
lower ~ higher ~ higher

The Hard Universe

A Snake living its natural life in the garden of Eden.
Thank God it was there to tell Adam & Eve to fuck.
"I'll believe it when I meet a talkin' snake"
They still don't believe the Earth is round.
Yet they know Adam & Eve had a wild fuck
& there's a talkin' snake of procreation ~
Power corrupts inside a Global hypocrisy.
'It's the most powerful but best kept secret'
A bullet-proof Pope-mobile when Jesus
wasn't afraid to be crucified was he?
Buddha used to beg for his food ~
He renounced the Golden Palace
and his devoted wife and family.

*

Just say the Truth

Planets are orbiting ~ we're merging into the future
Using Earth's gravity to shoot us out into Space ~
Words of enlightenment meeting in the One world.
Dreams becoming reality*Quantum*Leaping energy.
They lost, got stuffed, they napalmed them, still couldn't win!
Global MIC. Terror is Greed, endemic Corruption Mr. President.
What's it gotta do with the Syrians?
Wiped out a country that could
have brought the dollar down!
Blown up by an RPG on behalf
of his Capitalist democracy!

Choking on his Monster
The Mind's desires separated us not only
from the Supreme but from Y/ourself.
They got it from the Source
They had no separation ~
No Mind between them to separate them.
Maya coming, only she can get you in the mind.
The mind creates the mind that tells you
'You're Sunny Jetsun'
And that God is a separate entity.
The day you realise there is no separation ~
non enlightened Ego ~ You're truly enlightened.
*
Back in
the now ~
It's all gone
* Ultimately *
You're on your own
but part of the whole.
*
Power of Now
And get over yourself!
I had enough. A gypsy.
Want to settle down ~
Can't satisfy all the needs.
Sat in a meadow staring at hemp weeds.

His Heavy Shiva ling shank
Reaming True essence of who you are ~
You realize this is a complete Ocean
of devotional Love and compassion.
"You can't be arsed with anything!" said,
my psychedelic Hindu, mythology teacher.
He had to take care of the World.
Gods have Tigers to ride.

*

Scripts
Makes sense when all the Mandy's around
Heavily hypnotic losing the inhibition ~ free
Let's have a passionate orgy full of new energy.
Let's all become VIP Easy Riders…. Fat chance!
Love and Peace and Flower Power.

*

The Frame
Surrender to the present moment ~
And only focusing attention on that.
Just be presence not the hallucination.
Then you Love everything ~ You Love
Because You Are As It Is
Eternity in the Ego state
In the Illusion.

Clear Space

And it all gets fucked, turned into an oilfield refinery.
Enslavement in your mind, you can never get enough!
Identification with the Role models.
Missing real human aspects of life ~
A mental prison, shouldn't be arrested.
It's Conditioning from 1000's of years...
Up to 'This is MY toy.' Mine, Possession.
It's not the Object it's what's in your head;
It's not the ego's Illusion of Me & Mine....
Can't get it means we need more and more.
"I wouldn't be human if I didn't worry, sorry"
Turn it around and you'll get the truth of it!
Nothing more than perceiving my mental-space.
Missing the sacred forest*Human is to be Divine

*

Game of Tensions

Suffering over your Imagination ~
No fear or paranoia when you're in Love.
A mental delusion ~ thought in the body.
'You don't feel good, you're stressed!'
No end to the light at the end of the tunnel.
The light is the tunnel as the presence is now.
Not meditating on the doing but the being ~
"Let's have a war and make some money!"
'Shine light and people will find the path'

The Big Secret
"It's all in your head ~ Have it all.
You don't have to go anywhere to pray!"
They're robbing your energy.
India, "Unbelievable, full of surprises!"
Online pocket vagina on a key ring,
blow up doll on the passenger seat.
Anything can happen, look who's the head
Demon of the UN. Human Rights Council!
Not paid to think it's only for the money.
Explaining the Veda's Chaos Theory

*

Not a Parasite
A squaddie wired up!
That's why it's good to be a hippy.
Drop by if you're ever in Amsterdam.
'The Planet has All the answers'
He understands a black hole ~"Good for him"
It's Mind based not Nature based, needs R*evolution.
What might happen, I'm naked walking on a deserted beach
I see a beautiful, naked woman walking towards me, alone ~
will I turn into a beast? I didn't, it was super natural and cool.
Awareness of Awareness ~ really a message to the heart.
Naturalists "It's all an Illusion ~ but a nice one"
"If I'll be Tarzan will you be Jane?"

<u>Yama*Dhamma</u>
"Raging against the dying of the light"
Resisting nature ~ accept it and move on
with right intention. "Just don't wanna go!"
No choice ~ in the moment
Can't fight it ~ Surrendering
"You're going into Shock!"
You're in that right place.

*

<u>Be Happy</u>
Can do it anywhere ~
Don't need Speed dating.
Be happy with other people.
SIMPLE
An army of lunatics
The end of the world
for a lot of people.

*

<u>Rumi*Spacious</u>
Getting in that Sufi Open Space ~
Discernment is not Judgment.
'Awareness or Ideology?'
'We're Poisoning ourselves!'
You have only an opinion, it has value to you.
They don't necessarily have to be acted upon.
That's where the discernment comes in.
You can be challenged ~ Guilty by Association!
What happened to innocent until PROVEN guilty?
"I'm sure she's at her wits end in complete despair."
An innocent head under the gaze of Madame Guillotine!

<u>Bring Ball</u>
The most basic thing is to breathe ~
What's happening in this moment?
Not the moment ~ eternal space
of consciousness ~ surrenders.
Where it makes it happen.
Holy cow it's always now.
Hell is just my imagination.
Fear comes into the eyes
Obvious the true nature
of the Matrix..

*

<u>Broken Innocence</u>
Hardening her up to be like them.
They want respect, beg for forgiveness!
Invasion of the land of milk & honey ~
They built an electric fence of razor wire
How it works with the most powerful weapon!
'Love thy Enemy' ~ Transmutation
In that momentary feeling

*

<u>Transmuting*Seer</u>
Why're we sat here in this unconscious state, it's shit?
Changes happening in the Conscious space.
You can wake up from the unsatisfied mind.
Not promoting any war on the path of Jesus.
"I'm an angel deep inside me fallen in a place
where there is no dark or light.
When it STOPS being mental you are there
Because it's beyond the thinking mind ~

<u>What is that game?</u>
"You have to come back to Yourself
YES
Where else you gonna go?"
Put it into the subconscious
with no attachment.
Increasing your good karma
because there's nothin' out there mate.
*

<u>Classic Waves</u>
Between theta and delta
Materialising galaxies ~
Be Space behind everything
Allowing the results to appear
on the screen of your life.
Focusing your own AI. Intention.
Abundance of Life
doing a little dance.
*

<u>Breakfast at the Oasis</u>
Never invite suicide bombers to stay
Who's censoring alternative thinking?
Maybe they're trying to brake nature!
Not allowing for the opposite polarity ~
that's why the world is out of balance now.
'A Fascist Biological Di*magnetism Pretence'
Against gravity through ether the '5th element.'
Her pussy went down to the bottom of the shaft!
Should I let it go ~ just let it be...
Sublime, super*sensitivity is Free

Energetic Fields

Mandalas, Yantras are maps of the Universe
which we can't see. Ask at any Crop circle!
Otherwise what's the alternative?
ALWAYS HAVE AN OPEN MIND
Because they don't know either!
Rishis and yogis are not hippies.
......If you are FEELING IT......
Feelings running through the Pain.
We all dropped from the Ocean ~
Merging Finite with the Infinite

*

Flipping Out

They all wanna destroy the World!
They're doing it to themselves.
It just makes life fascinating.
Taste buds don't exist beyond the mind.
Wants a joint ~ Instant Rebirth!
'You have all the Freedom' Needs a chit?
Yeah, from an Ayurvedic doctor!
And it's Legal!

*

'If you believe in something

Got to put your cock on the block!'
Take them to the cliff top edge ~
they'll push backwards into you!
"Good smoke, Good Acid, Good Chicks."
"How many mushrooms we got in Wales!"
Have a good time.

A Special Friend

You're absorbing things making you feel good.
Attracting Apsaras at a full moon beach party.
'You're Not Rejecting her your journey together has ended!'
'She goes her way you go your way' As it is...
That heavenly feeling ~ between her legs.
"Without the Shiva ling the Yoni is useless."
You mean they don't enjoy it; They love it!
"She'll be your slave, save a lot of problems!
It's up to her she's not a Slave.
Slaves to Cocaine or another addiction.
If you have that in your pocket
then they're Slaves to you. Is that true?
Best lookin' women addicted to the Ego."
"I wouldn't buy a Slave I couldn't fuck."
"But I'd buy her and set her free ~"
Then she'll be enslaved by another,
so better keep her.

*

Self*Motivation

I just couldn't believe it that my deepest soul mate
could turn to be such a traitorous & ignorant villain!
'Give Peace a Chance mate' ~ Forgive if you can.
Don't know what they've done, at least they think so.
That's because they've never felt ~ their Inner Peace.

*

Anti*Polarity*Bi Polarity

A sort of beautiful Iranian hippie hybrid.
We all left our own cultures and countries.
When you look in the mirror it's up to you what you see

Bio*Prasad

Made energetic Love in an entheogenic garden.
"It's all OK." "Fuck me that looks a bit mad!"
All Presidents have been Ignorantly Unaware!
The establishment has robbed from the poor,
gave themselves all titles, not for any rebels!
Caught lorry load of explosives & 4 Mossad agents!
Controlling the people putting them in fear making
them Slaves. Using Fear Politics of enslavement!
Some care it's not all about the money but liberty!
Conditioning, Crime, Reward and Punishment.
That's why the Matrix System is run by Terror.
Celebration of yourself not only its acceptance.
Who has ever read 'The Politics of Ecstasy'?
"Wow that was so dreamy"

*

Be Friends

Who's laundering all that Nazi money?
Who the fuck wants war Herr Goering?
We forget it's a f.... movie.
Don't let it end bitterly.
We truly think it's real ~
We make each other
so 'Fuck it!'

*

Give Love
Give Kindness
Give Compassion
It's very simple.

31

Bondages of Reality

Part of nature, swimming in ponds where you'll be eaten.
Nature doesn't give a fuck about the colour of your door.
Man-made mental-constructs, "I lived with 3 dogs, 3 cats
one of them a bully in Gopal's kitchen during monsoon"
The spirit spoke to me and asked me a question...
Transmutes seeds, cheating wife been there done that!
More than words, from a higher perspective.
"I don't give a shit what Buddha said, how about Ego?"
We all bleed when they hammer the nails in our soul!
The white supremacists will take every last red cent!

*

Child born in the Spirit

"I'm interested in what is not what isn't" Transcends it!
"It's more than what you think" Violent since day one!
Be like puppets as long as you stay in that dimension.
Who's spending the most money on Killing people?
Who's making the most money from Killing people?
Gruesome Memory, "I'm backin' Putin, NWO. resistance!"
Who's supporting all these tyrannical demons?
Isn't it confusing who's pulling the strings
Comes in and out ~ who needs to survive?
Spiritual*being we were not cruel people.
Warriors don't slack off or lose your heads!
Flesh doesn't want to die, programmed to live.
"The tree of knowledge is death ~ the tree of life
Is beyond man's knowledge"

<u>*No Magic without the wand darling!*</u>
"They don't do the business they do the pleasure ~"
Insane Satanists they all lied to the World on WMD.
And the files can't be released for another 70070 years!
Believing in Father Christmas, is democracy Supermanic?
What the fuck, blurring our psychology making judgments!
Desensitising people, nameless faces, they're 'Our Enemies'
Making them exist, their justification for us giving the Scourge,
legitimate acknowledgement they're Aliens, representing Satan.
It's so blatant setting up exactly, limits of Psy Ops. Warfare!
Mass manipulation, understanding human nature, behavior.
They could change it but want it, which seems so fucked up!
Psychopathic power representing the Elites not those below.
Sick minds being channeled into Jihadis and their handlers.
Hopeless from permanent states of poverty and deprivation.
Demonising 'em trick, they're not humans with any feelings!
A hotel in Mali was shot up but not on any mainstream news!
Bamboozled & Hypnotised, "Man down, man down!"

*

<u>*"Are you gonna cum for me?"*</u>
"We swallow what we're given" What are they tellin' us?
Discerning how it stacks up against reality we're given?
"I want a Florentine Geisha from the hand of Bottichelli"
She'll serve you tea & ravioli as a happy Celebration!

*

<u>*Broken Kisses*</u>
Unholy land of Apartheid -
throwing stones at Tanks!
If someone's gonna kill you
You have to fight back!

<u>Deja vu ~ Deja vu ~ Deja-vu</u>
Time Traveller Tech, Ask at Project Ibis
Encoded his 13 strand DNA into a Tarot card.
"He sends me hearts when he wants some loving!"
Morphing*Integrating into a multi-personality ~
And wiping her mind clear of all thoughts of ETs!
Did you ever meet any Shadowy Government clones?
Yes easy to take your Soul put it into a High Vibration.
"Sorry but my hearts go to my Lover!"

*

<u>House of Despotic Swords</u>
Putting his neck on the block and a lot worse for criticising
Sordid Arabian Fundamental Theocratic Oligarchy.
A Crime of defiling God! How bad is it? Horrible, bigotry,
repressive supported by our collaborating Government.
Surveillance storing all our Metadata for a rainy day!
'Foundation for Free Speech/Expression.' Supporting ~
Raif Badawi, Saudi human rights blogger imprisoned &
Ashraf Fayad, Palestinian poet/artist sentenced to death!

*

<u>Perception under the Impression</u>
Coke, You feel your Ego is Supreme, where is your honour?
His Mahatma picture is on every wall, banknote and stamp.
"It doesn't mean anything, died by an assassin's bullet!"
He was a **F R E E D O M * F I G H T E R** Against fools
who wanted to Rule it all with their own God of E G O.
"They're sick of the British making new rules everyday!"
A bruised ego thrown off a train began a social revolution.
Blown Bose speaker, plane crashed, never found his body!

Which You Are

A stone creating ripples in your serene pond.
TTP. ~ means now Corporations can Kill you
And they can't be prosecuted only deregulated!
Why are they making more laws for us the people
and less laws for business? It's totally Unbelievable!
'Your Spirit is the most important thing in the Universe.'

*

The Big Secret

The Powers that be don't want you to know it ~
Your Vital Life Essence not Trans*humanism hybrids.
Artificial Intelligence is taking over our Natural Humanity.
Meet Infinite Jade, Master of the known Nanodata Universe.
Futuristic concepts making people into advanced machines.
All Propaganda- 'You'll do what you're F... told Program'
Who wants to eat today stand in line! ~ Martial Law....
"You got the Army calling the shots Colonel"
'Keeps 'em Rich!'

*

'AMABLE'

'It's simple
be nice ~
You know You Like It'

*

The Extreme Victim!

Take Away * Ego *Take Away * Tao
Surfing through the Light tunnel
Forgive them because they don't....
Happy with someone giving herself Love.
"Far out man, I'm fully feline pussy purring!"

<u>International Defenders of Human Rights</u>
Why does society allow for the persecution & prosecution
of the Truthsayers, from Socrates to Galileo & recently
Mohammed Ali, Elsberg, Assange Manning. Snowden?
These are the messengers describing to us the heinous
crimes of our leaders, whether Political, Religious, Social,
Corporate, Military etc. These crimes take all forms but
all of the perpetrators are allowed to escape investigation
and justice! The list is endless yet it is these messengers
of Truth who are allowed by us to be sacrificed! Ask Why?
'Edward Snowden took the morally courageous step to tell
the truth of Illegal Government activities at the highest level
of Intelligence taking away people's democratic rights. As a
whistleblower telling the World the truth (for which he has now
been vindicated by the US Appeal Court) he put his own life in
extreme danger as can be seen by what has happened to US
and other whistleblowers. They are then made to be seen as
the real criminals by these same Authorities' 'legalised' illegal
abuses of Power.' Here is a Prime example, made for us to
'see' these obvious Contradictions showing clearly their lies,
made to control our minds, bodies, emotions, psyches & spirits.
These people have made clear to us Governmental criminality
and corruption and they're now being imprisoned even though
they're acting on behalf of all of us! 'The Truth will set us Free'
which is the basis for all Democratic nations' rhetoric but it is
now Proven to be a SHAM! They don't want the Truth to unveil
their own treachery! Let us at least realise this and demand that
justice be served on these criminals, sociopaths and we realize
we're being enslaved inside a political, economic, military Matrix.

And to show this is a Global Political Corp. phenomenon
eg. in India it's used to Control people as anywhere else!
It's difficult to become AWARE of the ubiquitous Matrix net
and its malevolent consequences on our social lives and on
our perceptive levels of integration with nature but the signs
are clearly there. When Governments take such obviously
'Incomprehensible' actions against humans and nature then
these clear contradictions can then allow us to see the light
through the Mind-controlling, propaganda and brain washing.
These are precious moments for our 'Enlightenment' and are
to be 'Realised as such'. 'Authorities' banning of Greenpeace,
Oxfam, Amnesty International and any independent observers
of Governments are clear signs that they have something they
want to hide which is not in our interest. How can any of these be
legitimate when their people do not even have the basics of life
such as food, shelter, clean water, child care, security and Peace.
They can talk all they like about Economic prosperity, GDP political
freedom and the rest of it and WE should know that it's all lies,
illusions & bullshit. Awake and live our truths in spiritual solidarity!

*

Building a Church, RIP. Appeal
Jesus never said 'give me money
and I'll cleanse, take away your sins.'
The powers that be made the rules & laws.
Still believing they are going to Heaven!
"It's only the death of this person not YOU"
Only that rebirth, Identity, chance to become
I M M O R T A L

<u>*FREE*STYLE*</u>
WTF. Reacting with/out Aggression!
"I'm ready to meet someone else"
"I'm crying out for more"
Love listening to Sade,
'Your Kisses Ring, 'Your Love is King'
'Your Love Is/It's blissfully f.....' Real'
*

<u>*Out of Tune 'Hari Om No Telephone'*</u>
Government Science Focusing has got it all wrong.
A completely wrong Perspective for whose agenda?
Not seeing other States of Mind, same Consciousness
but as abnormal conditions, syndromes, unnatural ~
Gives them any reason to section you as Anti Social!
Keeping their Authority, criteria to enforce their rules.
They have the Power to exploit the holistic nature of us.
Defining You as Autistic, Anarchist anti person terrorist.
Sorry, children not playing in the street, fields any more.
They really have no Awareness of human Consciousness.
The blind leading the blind into violent oblivion!
On Presidential detail, good with a machine gun!
Painful Brain doing it for their own Mega Egos.
"I've asked the Gods to bless your sword mate"
"How soon do you march?" "Kill them all!"
*

<u>*"No he didn't suffer, he died instantly"*</u>
'Surely It must be better to live than to die?'
With more and more Heart breaking dreams!
Torturing yourself ~ Dying out of Love!

Venus*Aller*Retour
Your Ego's reasoning overpowered your Heart.
I'm in a vacuum, if you don't remember
what's the fucking point of being in love?
You gotta clear your head of that shit mate!
*Bewitched Space * My Love is Eternal.*
I'm very happy to meet you.
How deep do you want to go ~
How good is your true Telepathy;
Are you able to cross the Cosmic sea?
Being in adoration ~ timelessly with me.

*

Breaking the Blue Prints of Words
Emotionless not having any feelings or even caring.
Earth is an Encoded prison, our heart's unaware of it.
*Absorbing human energy*sources to higher realms.*
Where's the millions of missing, disappeared children?
"Be aware of these forces or stay asleep!"

*

The Sequencer
Keep your expectations to yourself!
"I don't hear the music ~I feel it!"
*Electronic computer, binary 1*0*
"The essence of the music is Space"
Listening to the Psychedelic Trans ~
end mental ~ 'I'm going for the music'

God Is the Boss
'The One & Only'
Jesus wasn't a Materialist, false witness or Jihadist!
He can't teach anything to them folks in Jerusalem.
Living in a madhouse; if you are innocent you can go.
Living with snakes ~ He wanted to Chelo the Planet.
He gave everything even that was misunderstood!
Three million Moslems killed, five million homeless!
The Bible doesn't teach that.

*

All the Wants
Life attuning me to the present moment ~
All those things in the Kingdom of Heaven.
Turn up and see it through transmuted eyes.
Through experience leading to total Acceptance.
Those believing, knowing, identifying with their perceptions;
What's the Mind telling you ~ is anything else going on?
Simply being

*

Dalai Lama
'As a human being I acknowledge that my well-being
depends on others and caring for others' well-being is
a moral responsibility I take seriously. It's unrealistic
to think that the future of humanity can be achieved on
the basis of prayer or good wishes alone; what we need
is to take action. Therefore, my first commitment is
to contribute to human happiness as best I can.'
Om Mani Padma Hum* * *VIVE L'AMOUR*

<u>On the Pope's call for Social Aide</u>
Same old Rhetoric* the Inquisition is always waiting round the corner.
It's over 2000 years since Jesus pronounced Love your neighbour
and despite the church being the Richest & most Powerfully,
obeyed Theo/Kleptocracy and Authority in the Visible &
invisible World throughout history we are still hearing
the same blah blah! Realise all these shrouded, secret
Contradictions and ask yourself what's really going on in
God's house and with its emissaries in these times of Gaia.

*

<u>CONTACT</u>
OBSERVATION IS AN ACT OF CREATION
(The Limitations Inherent in the THINKING//MIND EGO)
Being impelled to change rearranges the abstract
art into another layer of abstraction as a fractal
going deeper into creativity into this hologram ~
allowance being in the here and now in the timeless.
By giving me a name label you are negating all the other
aspects that I could be by creating the illusion of solidity
of a 'nature morte' portrait but this is alive in the moment ~
continuity changing Stream of consciousness so having
synchronistic authentic/intelligent, creative reality!

*

<u>Illusion Why Worry?</u>
If you can be happy in the present ~
You can be happy the rest of your life.
In the conditioned state all turning to dust!
'Our karma is our belief in past & future ~
Once you get rid of it you're out of karma'
Determined in the past*Projected into the future.

41

Koh I Noor

"It's God's diamond; 'Hari Krishna, Hari Rama.'
'Whoever shall own it shall own the World'
She has the Kingdom of heaven between her legs!
'Look at what women you got by your karmas!'
Shakti she can make your life or destroy it.
Taught her how to put a knife in his back!
The Powerful rule, they need a Goddess.
Kali is black ~ Cosmic Space

*

Full Nasha

"Cuddle me, kiss my neck ~
Bend over ~ at the Lolly Pop Shack.
"Every day I go out my door it's a new day"
"It's not a drug it's a medicine"
Delivered over the dark web.
"He owns the legal system!"
"There are holes in the net."
"Is that the one that fell down the steps?"
People being honest with themselves...

*

Lazy All Day

Where's today's philosophers challenging the status quo?
A soul without a body ~ use your Consciousness.
Shakti is the female*Universe is a Goddess.
They're crystals to me Baba in my reality!
Giving birth all the time to galaxies....
What's your word worth your Honour?
All the free-loading in their Constitution.
FREE IS FREE

Dank Ruby Dawn
Summer blue light streaming through
the cool Spaces of CHEFCHAOUEN.
God said "Love your Enemy" and I obeyed
him and loved myself" ~ Khalil Gibran.
Be Divine not a Psychopath*Anonymously.
Nuclear weapons are a Crime Against Life!
Everything is good; I need to go to Tibet......
Lhasa in January under her blood red Moon.

*

Dr. K & Mr. Smiley Ensemble
Are you looking for a little plastic bag with drugs in it?
"I don't need to go walkin'
I spend 30hrs a week on the dance floor."
We know what happens when the Gestapo
S.S. knocks at your door!
Believed in his Divine Right to be King.
A Holy fucking Tyrant not a man!
"You've lost the feeling with someone you know."
'When it's the closest people to you, you stab in the back!'
Human being, Spirit being, flowering in life.
Litres of Ketamine just off Pushkar Square.
How the f.... do you drum on that?
That's a path I never went down.
Poisoning our children's future!
A marvelous thing bio*chemistry.
The white lady opening her wings.
Dancing with your foot chopped off.
You'll like it; What does it really mean?
"You can't fuck me!"

<u>Higher*Consciousness*Permanent ~ Impermanence</u>
'Don't aspire to make Samadhi states Permanent because
they don't sit so well with the many practical tasks
we all need to attend to...' because there's
no permanent state only the ever changing ~
Cosmic essence which is in tune with higher
consciousness which is ultimately ~ 'Who'
we are and we can get fully distracted by
these attachments of Mind/ego, the tasks
of karma*dharma*panorama*life until we
are trance*mitting*receiving*trans*muting
loving empathy & we begin to dance.
*

<u>PLANETE*PARADISE</u>
SATELITE CONSCIOUSENSES
SPIRITUAL * NEOCORTEX
HIGHER KARMA OF DEEPER LOVE
THE SEAT OF THE FOUR SUBLIME STATES
COSMIC*METTA*KINDNESS
LISTENING TO THE SOUNDS
FEELING THE FLOWING ELECTRONS
TRY IT WITH YOUR EYES CLOSED
SITTING In the OPEN HEART
of a 1000 PETALED LOTUS
*

<u>of It</u>
In it, on it, and out of it!
Everything's easy why..
Am I suffering?

Fast Forward Revelation
Spirit rising, Pink Spaceships coming down!
Broken heart, "I put all my Trust in someone"
Ego gone mad, caught in her hot root chakra ~
No emotional response, if you're lucky you'll
discover it but some people never do!
"Oh I've been cut off – Totally Crazy!"
It's about what you gonna do Now
with all your unique experience?
The Secret ~ Never Stop!
*

Christ Son of Krishna
In Holland there is no drug paranoia!
'The Absolute 3 minutes Chakra test!'
Different levels of feeling
Love uniquely ~ together
being here now forever.
"Even I got a breaking Limit"
*Limitless ~ He's found Love!
'The Gods are with us ~ of course!'
*

Agnostic Bio*tech
'You're infinite consciousness*experiencing being human'
Who was spinning deadly GMO trails all this time?
Lying in blazing sunbeams, what's better than that?
Black shadows ~ "I got my Space gun down there"
Shooting all the bubbles, we're coming from Stars.
Watching from the Ghats at Varanasi during Arti.
Painting a Mandala ~ 'Chai, chillum, chapatti.'
Adoration of the golden Planet.

<u>Mystical Magus</u>
The Secret Teachings
Pythagorean Theorems
Restoring us to Paradise.
Imprisoned for suspicion of Sorcery
Occultist*Communicating with Angels
Excommunicated from the body of Christ.
I felt guilty to leave, she taught me to be free.

*

<u>Holiday Camp</u>
Who's the Dalai Lama?
Interpreting it has to make sense.
Focusing on doing what you like.
Mermaids in all my dreams

*

<u>This Epic Journey</u>
Manipulation APP * A Jaded Supercomputer.
We know exactly what they're doing
We don't care ~ Brainwashed Mind.
Creating a Whole New Dimension.
All news is fabricated, green screen Illusion!
What about the frequency affecting ~
Feelings are transient ~ but they're what we live for.
'Soapy Massage*Where the customer comes first!'
"I didn't know that but it explains a lot"
Don't get caught up in that shit.
'The end doesn't justify the means' ask karma.'
"I'd rather just give something to someone"

Kamashakti Labium Day
*"On a different path ** wish her luck!"*
Don't shit on people, gotta live your own Life.
"I got no money so she can never give me respect."
Isn't that funny if it's true?

*

Under Duress
"I don't consent to being stopped speeding!"
"Your Machine is not Full Proof to a free man"
Asserting your Common law Rights mate.
"It's Not his job. You haven't committed a crime."
It's all deception and Fraud me Lud!
How much is the Pope, Queen, King of Sordid Arabia,
Dubai, Shanghai, Mumbai plus the Rothschilds' worth?
'Want to know what it is in the world we're so mad about.'
'Science, whether they believe it not ~ it's still there.'
You can't be Infinite ~ if you're incarnated you die.
*It burns your nerve*universe system, dying of fright.*
Not for Shiva the Lord of manifest Timelessness.
He takes no shape ~ he is never born.
The Universe is always changing

*

Your favourite Geisha
"I don't have to go that far
I'm already in Heaven"
They all glow in the dark.
Others want everyone indebted.
You are here as a Cosmic Being

Leviticus Servitude
'Weekly Female Slave market and it's been Ordained!'
Go and be a whore and buy a small farm if got luck.
"I'll keep the love going on forever ~" It's all a concept!
"Women today don't need men anymore, superfluous!"
"Sperm is the most important thing in the Universe"
International Pleasures in the House of the Setting Sun.

*

Top Twerk
"Where's the nearest slave market on rue Prince Ali?"
'A Flower Child Time Travelling through Space
with Nothing but Respect, Love & Trust'
Happiness*smiling through your*her eyes
HAREM NIGHTS INCORPORATED

*

Staining Glass
It's all about understanding the weightless Mind ~
You're not going to give any of it away to the poor
might as well have an orgy, bring me the slaves!
Put a Lion's head on the wall as a trophy kill,
the last Black Rhino's horn down your pants.
Worth more than Gold on the Hang Seng.
Church the biggest hypocrites going!
Always got your horny Alpha males
Gyrate that skinny, bony ass Baby!

*

Love Stems
The ultimate Maya *I love Orchids
Bathing naked in Serotonin
Pagan women dancing around a fire

Everyone wants to get smashed!
Being with someone you wanna be with ~
And they wanna be with you because they love you.
In Cambodia yur in the shower before yu know it!
Hard to resist, she's gorgeous, random meeting in a bar.
"I can live with small tits, with nice nipples!"
"I was interested because of her interest"
"Let's all fuck off to Phnom Penh!"
Babe sat on your lap every night.
"I like to give good head massage"
Just to give people something
makes them laugh and shine.
"I felt really at home there"
Smiling into her eyes.

*

Random*Evolutionary
In its DNA to have wings but not switched on ~
Why a hedgehog, why an Armadillo and ants?
All these animals coming down together
and making room for other animals.

*

It's not Rocket Science
Space is formless can't know it with Mind's finite perceptions.
What's the Battle of Waterloo gotta do with price of fish?
How to get people to live together without killing anyone.
What's your idea of creating Eden? 'Chicks love to fuck;
Heaven on Earth they give birth, they give pleasure.'
"Don't believe in your own bullshit or you'll be hurt!"
Almost every day something Spectacular happens.
Jumping up and down, more energy in the dance.

<u>Shiva Prasad with Brahma Kumaris</u>
Tourist Wallah sitting at the big banyan tree. A naked Nagar
Baba is legally allowed to carry ½ Kilo of charas in India.
"You mess with him you're dead, drinks pani from a skull!"
'Lying on a bed of nails ~ he'll get up for a chillum!'
"They haven't figured out where I come from yet!"
Psychedelic Interpretations of an Indian puppet show.
The music has to talk to you ~ it makes you fly
There's nothing like a good Psy*trance party ~
The music has to make you swim in the dream.'
Fractal seeds within a sprouting consciousness.
You feel the vibe ~ the energy in that.
Music makes you smile.
*

<u>Creative Jinns</u>
'Women have brains ~'
Chicks and water nymphs
they came lusting after him.
Woman is Alive ~ good to know.
All that hanging about wanting to get into you.
You are a Bottichelliette of the ferns inside that forest.
Who said that **'Grass is greener where you water it'?**
"I wanna eat some Kashmir musk, from her spice souk".
We always want what we don't have SYNDROME ~
'You're not rich til you got something money can't buy'
Do you believe in yourself? Ultimately I trust myself!
Pulling you into temptation, the full seductive Maya.
'Temptation is Illusion' ~ but we believe it.
The Cosmic Rishi lost all his powers to her wiles.
Reaching the Heavenly Planet.

Shri Mantra in the Jungle

A Magical number of faces ~
Connected to Shiva with my Rudraksha beads.
Has to Believe in the Power ~ the cradle of **Magic**
Is Alive Woman Is Magic*I Am Magical too.
'Within each of us there is a mini Universe'
Give a girl an apple and see what happens!
In a dream, what to do about the 7 chakras?
Pulling a Jinn in from another dimension ~
He's screaming no one can hear him in a bottle!
Weird and wonderful*Aliens in everything!
What a killer Dosa!

*

In the meantime

Holding your Lotus shining in the dark with your light
Why are we not spinning when the world is spinning?
Good question ~ Live like there is no tomorrow..
Raising your Kundalini absorbed in Tantric Heaven.
You can do what seems like magic but you're just Free!
Sexually I'm creating life not doing anything wrong.
Using Mantras "I believe in Aliens*I've seen UFO's"
Who is the Devil, fallen demons dancing around him?
"I'm not afraid of the dark ~ or my own shadow!"
We're surrounded by Angels being in the light
"So why worry enjoy the dark side and come back"

*

Enjoy be Happy

Make a nice thought what else you gonna do?
Relaxing sunbathing by the sea with my. No. 3.
"I am a little devil I don't have to wear a horn!"

Living with People
She was pure pleasure a complete delight
"Gotta lotta Love Baba"
About real deep experiences.
A Paradise Paradigm shift ~
Happy & free to do what you like.
Lingering Love, it's about ME
My Love is what I want to be.

*

"No happy end to Love ~ Is there ever an end?"
"He just wanted to keep enjoying fucking her (to death)!"
She lets me die without a word, without flinching a muscle!
Without a sound or a whisper not even one tear just nothing!
Passive aggressive appears to her as normal circumstances.
In full denial, rejection of the strongest, best lover she ever had!
Stuck a Psyche knife in the heart of a soul mate, no remorse!
How can someone do that? Borderline Personality disorder.
I know from Love we shared that it's completely unnatural ~
Shocked! She made a choice never to see me ever again!
Where are your feelings, empathy, compassion, humanity?

*

Selfish destruction*Mantra
Having only the greedy feeling for money.
Making the right programming, protocols.
Cold hearted, never guilty, no heart or soul.
Doesn't give a fuck but that's your big lesson.
"She's fucked it off, it doesn't work!"
The rest of the world is paying the price!
"I'm healthy, dynamic and fully Alive!"

<u>Lover's Love</u>

Argh! "She didn't do it to you, you did it to yourself!"
Your anger & hate killed it, me, us so many times.
Betrayed, knocked it on the head, smashed it.
Cruel, watching, letting it slowly drown alone.
Strangled it, tortured, suffocated, stabbed it...
in the back, in the chest, in the throat, in the heart.
Filled it with your poisonous curse, no Compassion!
Just selfish, greedy, jealous, Ignorant, unconscious Ego.
Heaven or Hell ~ All in y/our own Mind!
Real feelings ~ Who really knows why?
Letting me die, didn't give it any life!
'Love ending all the Madness'
'Men are emotional types'
"You can be so Heartless"

*

<u>PEACE NOT WAR</u>
RELAX & BE HAPPY
'Your thoughts are your own!'
What's rattlin' round in you...
isn't happenin' ~ to anyone else!
We're already there what you gonna do about it?
Fully trusting each other & you come inside.
People don't get it ~ we're all hypnotised!
"FUCK YOU!"

*

<u>Fast riches in every corner!</u>
What's he doing dangling outside the window
at the Queen's Palace escaping with no clothes on?
"People who cheat seem to succeed in this life" he said.

53

Hardest part of being a parent is watching a child go through something really tough and not being able to fix it for them
*These are the biggest lessons to have to finally surrender to and let the Universe take its course giving up our controlling/parental part of the situation and have faith knowing that our most beloved will survive and will come through with light shining & a big Smile wiser in their own knowledge of their deepest selves from this experience. When we're dealing with outside forces which seem so closed, cynical, ignorant, prejudiced and uncaring who have the Power to change things with a nod or signature or realisation of the Truth, or more time spent on getting the right medicine or the next piece of the factual evidence. We are put into their hands and often they fail thru greed, hate, lack of interest, corruption, misunderstanding. These dark nights of the soul can break our heart, take us to the limits of our Mind, show us parts of Spirit we never knew we had! Fear can fill the darkness and we feel completely alone ~ depressed often surrounded by people who are seemingly enjoying their own lives oblivious to what else is happening around them! We look into the eyes of these fellow humans and wonder WTF. is really happening as we feel so isolated! A friendly 'Human' gesture can make all the difference to people suffering in these circumstances. Every day such painful events occur... in Nepal, Syria, the village down the road, to a girl next door, the fear of losing our most loved ones! Friends who care and love you will do their best holding up the light in the darkness is life saving & gives us courage to carry on. It gives us the strength and inspiration to go to the deepest point within ourselves and be at the core of self realization * Hari Om*

MACROSPHERE*EQUATION

Tuning out a collapsing White dwarf Orb.
Empty full of frequency ~ Quantum Space
"We're living at the other end of the Rainbow"
"All matter is energy moving, condensed
to a slower material vibration"
Invisible microbial multi-dimensions ~
Dogons sun worshipping sky dragons.

*

Crashing Our Dimension!

Natural roots entwined in the wall of proven Science.
"Otherwise we'd all be walking around in the dark"
Changing the fabric, making your own Reality!
They manifested as travellers from Sirius
Came through an Opened Stargate ~
When did they first print Plato?
'The Directions to Atlantis'

*

Discern La Luz

Matter having an imagination of ourselves.
The key to opening the Portal into Space ~
Not seeing a light spot on the Moon's disc.
'ISIS> Israeli Secret Intelligence Service'
Pol Pot x 10,000, they're bombing empty sand!
"He took the ketamine drink by mistake, she had the acid and I
gave 'em the hash I'd held in my hand during a 3 month coma"
Reality is being portrayed on a green screen.
Having a dialogue with magic mushrooms.
DNA genetically programmed nature.
Without trees there is no Oxygen!

Silky Anti*Venom
'Check the expiry date!'
The Biggest Bull on Anjuna
beach dancing to Psytrance.
Sitting on an organic cushion ~
Cosmic natural static energy fields
being held in from Earth's gravity.
Can't pull out what you're receiving.
Yantra Free from Mind, body & 'I Am'
Not being disturbed*Tantra*Mantra*
*

Naked Inner detachment
They're talking about other energy.
~ Nine months in the devoted womb ~
You've even forgotten your past lives!
A Krishna picture with a lotta chicks.
There's not one Temple to Kamadeva.
The best kept secret in town...
*Is it all just an Illusion Baby*
Cosmic creation of birth ~
A drop fell out from Vishnu.
*

Chaste or not?
He let them tie him to a tree!
I wanna be carried away, drama free!
Praying to go back into Mother Earth.
The warrior's genes are still fighting.
"Lived with a demon can she be pure?"
She had to walk through the test of fire.
"How could you doubt me?" She was hurt

KALI

She's Mother Nature
when Space is Angry!
Cuts your Ego*head out.
The Ugly female demon
destroying the whole World!
Stole the fruits of our Lotus ~
Otherwise she's Queen Parvati.
Spellbound by proper Magic
*

Drug Rap

There's a lot of fake Police!
"I'm better than that"
In the War everyone's doing
what they're told or they're Shot!
A Lion eating an Antelope, natural instinct.
Athena shaking a Spear at the Ignorant Dragon!
If it has to happen it will happen ~
The Key, to see through the bullshit.
Surreal, Sublime * Peak your Power!
*

Anti*Matter*Cupids

No beginning ~ No end
Eternally*Infinite
Pure nature Parvati beside her
Lord of Material manifestation;
Destroyer of God's Ego ~ Time.
In Vishnu's Spiritual Universe.
Krishna the All Inclusive

<u>Expansion of Species</u>
That little bird that doesn't do
what it's supposed to do ~
That's how Nature works.
Lost his wings, people
put down and slaughtered!
Those that can get up get up!
The Program that has always been there.
Wanting to live in the Transcendent*LOVE
In resonance ~ everything is relevant
like a blade of grass.
*
Nature breezing through us in Goa ~
'We are the children of the R*Evolution'
the 10% not brainwashed, black sheep!
Your code is in every cell of your body;
DNA. Fractals, we don't know much.
'Fluoride is good for your teeth' Ad..
"We're under chemical/psyche Warfare"
Mass human consciousness will
f... over those Tyrant Controllers.
*
<u>Universal*Elements</u>
'In the Matrix * Know thyself'
'They Can't Control Everything'
Making us susceptible to the Alien
Transmission ~ Listening to it once,
the Programme loop is in your head.
There's this Love between people.
Subconscious

Cathedral of Freaks

"Gorgeous but no more, now full of tourists"
10 Kms country ride, you're seen as an Alien!
"At night you gotta be careful of the black cow!"
If you worry you miss the smell ~
No feeling of the senses you're not
Living ~ being in the moment.
Animals sit around all day doing
nothing why shouldn't we?

*

Mandala*Poetry

The point in the centre of the Universe
Illusions orbiting around a central Sun
Human consciousness and its Surreality.
Dreaming with the Imagination of duality
Expressing Nature through Love inspiration.
Awareness of the heart transcending phenomena.
On a Planet of Information overload

*

JADE PRISMS*BLUE BEAMS

The Investigatory Powers Bill
Structure of oversight verifying
the legality of their actions...
Google NSA & Secret courts
Links from the Inquisition..
Always done it, thinking it
Is their God given right!
"Who is a traitor, who is telling
the people the whole truth?"
Asking for Real Revelations.

He was a Pit Painter
I have a light in my heart
I was born with this light
This light shines through me
Because of this light I am
not afraid of anything.
Are you up for it?
*

Plinths
Welcome Home ~
No house is perfect.
Leaving deep empty Spaces
inside the Temple columns
for old time's sake.
*

I Am a FREE Man
"I've not been with a woman for a while!"
This ain't cool, Your heart's not happy.
She can't drown ~ Very funny bitch...
so full of plastic surgery!
Just means I'm not the same as you.
You gotta be willing to grow....
Chanting with 500 people
*

We got away with it!
The closer you come ~ the more we share.
Top quality Chinese balloons in Cambodia.
Feel the Sun the Best Feeling in the World.
A soundtrack of Confessions

*FOR ALL THOSE CRAZY LUNATICS OUT THERE ONLY CAUSING PAIN SUFFERING AND DESTRUCTION TO MOSTLY DECENT INNOCENT PEOPLE WHICHEVER SIDE YOU ARE ON WHICHEVER GOD YOU BELIEVE IN REALISE YOUR ACTIONS ARE INSANE AND IT IS TIME TO STOP IN THE NAME OF LIFE HUMANITY AND PEACE. YOUR MIND HAS GONE MAD AND THOSE WHO LEAD YOU DOWN THIS PATH ARE SOCIOPATHS. THERE IS NO TRUTH TO YOUR ACTIONS YOU ARE SIMPLY ENJOYING BEING HOMICIDAL MANIACS, THERE IS NO REWARD IN HEAVEN FOR SUCH BARBARIC BEHAVIOUR TO OTHER PEOPLE WHO LIVE ON THIS PLANET.
YOU ARE CREATING A HELL. WHY?*

*

*A Petition-on 'Wales Allowing Syrian Refugees'
to use Vacant holiday homes (fb Sept 2015)*
Somehow I don't see the local boyos going for that although I might be wrong and what about those 1 million holiday homes along the Arabian gulf? Direct in line to Mecca, better conditions and same law & customs! SERIOUSLY shouldn't this extremely desperate situation be dealt with properly by STOPPING these MANIACS who are Funding, supplying and Brainwashing ISIS and causing this genocide to their brothers & sisters? If it is the USA; Zionists, UK; Saudi Arabia, Qatar, illuminati, Military Industrial Complex, Oil Companies, Men in black or ETs make them take Responsibility! Someone's directing this; What are their fucking names & addresses, get me their files!

SHIVA*SHAKTI*ESSENCE

Everything has Spirit * One Consciousness ~
one vibratory force field. Through you*in you.
Looking out of every eye * * each particle
In the beginning was the LOGOS
not the word but the unknowable from which
the unmanifest becomes manifest, unconcealed truth.
'God is vibrating everywhere witnessing consciousness'
World's ever changing ~ collapsing into nothingness.
Animated Earth, sounds; patterns, vibrating water ~
Crystal human body... nature's drive to equilibrium, the
Unknowable, Divine *creation *principle is everywhere.
Imbued with pulsation Shakti moving Shiva Yin Yanging.
The root level fields of change ~ 'Anicca' impermanence.
When mind is more concentrated, free of Attachment ....
knowing existence. Through being Meditation, observing
subtler sensations * energies* continuously channeling
the story Inside us is the Universal.

*

Topped Himself

"Who's getting the most cash out of it?"
Arms sales up! Big Ego's looking for
satisfaction and still wants more
and more of the lush paranoia!
"It's a cruel world, I'm past it,
can't be bothered anymore."
It's really what's inside me.
Appearing as infinite creativity
Everything is a Form of Life ~
Manifesting 'the Universe'

<u>LOVELY * ENERGY</u>
Total Immersion ~ Engagement.
Tough Love Affirmation
Help us to Remember ~
"What do You want to Know?"
I RECEIVED THE GIFT
FULFILL*TRANSCEND
ALL OF THE SENSES*PEACE OF MIND.
'PLEIADES SPACE MOTEL, LEMURIA SPA
ATLANTIS ASHRAM, AKASHA RESORTS.
Started as a Literary fiction in time the ideas caught on'
Not expecting an arrow in the neck from a long distance
high velocity crossbow fired by a savage predator!

*

<u>Being Reborn</u>
Energetic ~ Meditation In the Temple of the Heart.
Without suffering the conscience can't be opened.
The key to Opening the door of your soul.
Always giving the benefit of the doubt!
'Fine Amor' ~ In relation to Humanity.

*

<u>VIVA LA VERITE</u>
In that picture you are the future ~ now ~ from the past
These 'Global Multi-national corporations' are doing what
good capitalists are brainwashed to do, that is to monopolise
VITAL resources whereby supply and demand dictate huge profits.
Tata , Kingfisher, Coca Cola, Pepsi, Nestle etc; all the same mindset!
Deaths of Journalists telling the truth about the World's Exploitation!
Galileo woke up and found the rest of the world asleep.

Trance Baby's Heartbeat 140*bpm
Oscillating higher frequency from Space
Top of the Psychedelic vibe ~
FEELING INSIDE YOU
Opening the Receptors
Keeping 'em Open
You Know ~ without words
Codes hidden in the sound.
DNA. tuned ~ you either get it
or you don't
*

Collective
'I AM' ~ It's Not In/divi/dual
We Are ~ Connected.
Psy*music, they get it,
go partying, it's a virus.
Opening the door
*

Please Apply.
'Illusion requires belief that thoughts in our head are us'
Making a Clean Mind ~ floating through history.
'Spacemen are coming back to say 'Hallo'
"Who's gettin' it?"
Sharing the native Kama Sutra of the Pleiades ~
'The Fall-Out's coming from their Sun Ray Guns!'
Lines of Cosmic radiation burnt into the grass.
Duality balloons flying to the Outer limits ~
And beyond.

<u>Heart Centre Rebalancing</u>

'True wisdom is accepting the potential that everything that you think you believe in may in fact be completely false.' "But there is the wisdom*that everything happening is to be transcended."

*

<u>Rapper Baba</u>

"She shagged me to death" ~ with a big grin on his face.
It'll take your mind off it, you're another happy madman.
"Keep God in your heart, thank him for the orgasm!"
Be mindful concentrate on the dhamma, do it yourself.
Golden cage, iron cage, they're both cages!
Duality Prison, both important for the Truth
They're suffering and they want holy revenge!
"I want to be at one with the Ocean. Eternal bliss
Sat Chit Ananda" ~ "All the rest is Illusion"

*

<u>Wikipedia   'Passive-Aggressive Disorder'</u>

*'May stem from a specific childhood stimulus (e.g alcohol/ drug addicted parents) in an environment where it was not safe to express frustration or anger. Families in which the honest expression of feelings is forbidden tend to teach children to repress and deny their feelings and to use <u>other channels</u> to express their frustration. **Passive aggression** can also be seen as part of a larger umbrella of hidden anger stemming from ten traits of the angry child or adult. These traits include making one's own misery, the inability to analyze problems, blaming others turning bad feelings into angry ones, attacking people, **lacking empathy**, using **anger to gain power**, confusing anger with self-esteem, indulging in negative self-talk. Lastly, the authors point out that those who hide their anger can be nice when they wish to be.'*

that sometimes these rigid, basic forces have some power over us...and any system does. I'm now in between the UK and Europe trying to decide which place in the World to put roots, where the best system has less demands even when I die! They strangle us and control us at every turn by their very nature and so WE have decided - to be free of it as much as possible. BUT in some cases they catch us because we fell into their trap or were put into their Matrix unsuspectingly.' The World is full of 'victims' as we know. It's for us to stay above it, to be Universal whatever they throw at us. Nailing the best to a cross as an example or this Saudi blogger who is getting f....d for asking for some basic human rights or those innocent people in Bangkok blown up yesterday! Or more 'mundane' stuff that is this covert, criminal poisoning of our environment ~ Ignorance par F.... Excellence. Even with someone we fall in love with they too can betray our trust! 'Dukkha' or their love is used by others to weaken us! The Universe is telling us to be* *Universal* regardless of the shit of these ignorant people with their stupid laws! You are doing everything you can and so is Kali to come out of this Black hole. There is even crazy 'realism' to it in the sense it is existing as a 'negative' but we have to transmute it with our truth and light whatever it takes to be free. We have to apply Love * Power*focused attention on these closed-minded people to break their Matrix! Yes ~ we're estranged from their small world but our bigger positive intention will force this Mind-Fearing to collapse! We just keep focused on this here and now ~ be patient!
Don't forget you are not alone*Love*Light*

<u>High^Attitude^Trust</u>
Mother Earth is having a heart attack, cardiac arrest!
Thank you for always accepting me into your family.
Not telling me to leave the house by 11pm.
Not like before, our all night Love in there.
All I gotta do is buy a ticket for me & you.
*

<u>NUDITY*T'ART</u>
More Rats than Cats.
Crazy crazy, to be free
and to do what you want!
Locked in * causing sensation
Nirvana or not, God or you/still breathing ~
We're Cosmic energy within a human Fantasy.
F... he don't believe we ever landed on the Moon!
Brought up on Science Fiction comics
'Observers of Planet Earth on Acid'
But it's still more separation and division.
Feeling duality <:> fighting unity Singularity.
'The Stranger in a very f.....' strange Land'
*

<u>Dalai Lama Satellites</u>
'Love is no Judgments'
Ask the 'Warlords of Mars'
Brought us this Reality ~ being here now.
I'm going with Sitting Bull, the Lakota Sioux.
What you goin' to make of this Book of Life?
It opens on a different page every day ~
Learning the lesson or not about Karma.
'Be happy have a Happy thought!'

<u>Glory Hole Smile</u>
Video Category: Blowjobs.
Who's going all the way down?
They've all got Swiss gold watches!
People will pay good money to see
gorgeous young women sucking Cock.
She really wants to make you a lot harder!
Her licentious tongue moving everywhere ~
Eating, devouring each other up voraciously.
Undress me, fingering her nubile ~ steaming wet slit!
Softly licking her labial lips, stroking her throbbing clit.
Fucking her mouth & arse, deep throating to the end...
She enjoys the sensation of a triple penetration explosion!
Excited shaved pussies' bedlam, facials, long brunette hair.
"Are you gonna cum over me?"
Snorkeling up the tight Vulva.
*

<u>The actor in the mask</u>
Bhakti*Transforming ~ Shakti women around Inspiring PEACE.
Make the most of the pain awareness sensation, it won't last.
Making another separation, dual judgments, ordained or not.
Earth is a round, flat, atomic disc spinning around the Sun!
Connections, Yes she'll have a bag of pure weed for sure!
*

<u>Odyssey an Epic Post Modern Prophecy</u>
Neural pathways Optimal*Telepathy enhancing Memory
for Time Travelling in your Mind through Cosmic Space.
Seeing the future & past together dancing in harmony.
My Magical-Realism*Surreal*Psychedelic Zen Poetry.
It doesn't matter if they get it; I get it sitting in a garden!

Spell*binding*Hot*Spot

"There was something manifesting and the fish knew it ~"
People felt safe so they returned to see the devastation!
Tumbling tumbling tumbling ~ spinning you more faster.
Half the island was destroyed in three minutes flat!
Holding onto a coconut tree, desperate to not let go.
"Sending prayers to all the family, this is the way I die!"
All of a sudden we popped up in the middle of the Ocean!
Now we all know what a Tsunami looks like.
She thought it was a Terrorist Attack!
Screaming ~ "I Love You!"

*

Temporal Mechanics

DNA. implanted into a Test tube
What is the future of the Universe? Turn Rt. at Area 51!
Ask the Galactic Federation Babes in Nautilus off Jupiter
Humanoids, reptoids, insectoids, Gravitation Coefficient?
Ask Psyonic with 2 hearts in the Secret Space Program.
What is the most important information held at this time?
Ask the 'Mars Colonisation Corporation' for a True quote.
Join Super-Soldiers before Trauma based Mind-Control.
Ask about Genetically engineered Project Moon shadow.
Awake travelling, more memories, being on a No Fly list!
Imprinted for the Astral Monarch Mission.

*

ZENDAO

'The word Art never came up in our house
for the first twenty years.' But it had Heart!
Never Surrender! Surrendered ~ Serendipity

Shouting like Canaries

Now 'Intellectual Terrorism' is dissonance.
Tuning into their own Love Consciousness ~
Starting to see fear, injustice and inequality.
3rd chakra anger and rage fighting over a bone!
"Me and you are gonna be one of the first to go!"
Oh a modern day witch hunt coming up.
Mark my words * the genius of illusion.
Making us believe it's 'All a lovely day.'
Welcome drones, total apocalypse on the way!
Advertising the 3rd world war; Back to the dustbowl.
Rejected out of hand perfectly received new information.
Familiarising them with the concept of Democratic society.
Aimed at Governments not distraction amongst 'emselves.
She's not a barmy old bag!

*

The Disaffected Herd

Another State of Emergency for National Security.
They are free to do what they want to anyone Lord!
Martial Law no more Social Liberty at the Bastille.
War necessary evil, realise perpetrated by the Military.
Power structure, industrial complex designed for Profit.
Dissidents escape in maintaining your higher vibration.

*

Cosmic Easy Rider

'Take a load of drugs ~
and go to Burning Man'
When I was in Love with ~
The bluest skies * shining in her eyes.
'So long sweet Marianne ~

Totally Alien Nandi
In the meditation dimension
The termites ate the floor ~
The Unbelievable ADHD. Indian bullshit dimension.
Like Japanese ants not understanding each other.
Using your mind's eye taught me the Shakohachi.
Taught to be contemplation ~ how to still my mind.

*

Speaking Spirit
Tongues of women ~
And tongues of Angels.
Messengers with blissful kisses.
The last time ~ now I know better.
Bubbles have a tendency to burst!
I'm at Peace ~ I walk away from it.
He became the leader of his church.
Killed his wife and murdered his son!
Guard your heart.

*

Conspiracy*Theory
Mr. Shakespeare, "We did go to the Moon"
Anyone says we didn't is a crank! Officially.
Used to be called FREE THINKING
Now it's 'New Intellectual Terrorism'
Dissidents executed in Saudi Arabia,
coming soon to your home town mate!
Let's communicate thru the 5th chakra.
It's Higher Level Stuff.

<u>Les Punatics</u>
"Just wanna have fun, be happy!"
"You know what I found out?"
"I Love duality"
'The straw that finally broke the camel's back'
Ego crossing the Mind's blue beam stream dimension
with the Unconscious, crazy parrot on your shoulder.
You can't possess the Magic in her eyes.
It's what you've got in your heart.
*

<u>Took out my Gandhi blanket</u>
Dzogchen Ponlop Rinpoche:
"From the point of view of Mindfulness
we all have Attention deficit disorder."
"I'm too old to give a fuck about anything now"
"Who knows the Apps. for prices of meteorites?"
"I can keep my Spirit up"
In a Stress Free Zone.
*

<u>Pink Peppers</u>
The Slapstick hookah lounge on midnight's deserted beach.
"No one spikes anyone anymore, it's too expensive!"
Realising we're the cause of our own suffering. Who else?
"It's gotta be a heroin addict, the only one got the balls!"
No guilt, no judgments it's all perfect.
"If they got it and they bight it ~
you got a good chance of getting it!"
Parvati ~ You feel like dancing

Why are you fighting Maya?
"Do you think he wrote all those books in Tibet ~"
based on what he said or other's interpretations?
Buddha isn't Buddhism, the church is nothing like Jesus.
The Jesuit, Roman Catholic religion designed Christianity.
"Enjoy your freedom ~ I'm into a truly FREE me.
Half your stress is gone ~ Singularity up again.
Here to Re*Mind you that existence is changing
You have to be the change even if it hurts ~
Don't be stuck in the PAIN, the nostalgia of Love.
You have to Remember the Pain that came with it.
The exit was suffering you don't wanna go through
that again do you? Don't be entrapped by games.
Sent by nature she's not waiting for you is she?
Don't be stuck, living in the PAST, not happening.
Now in the Present ~ No Heart Feelings.
Not putting any energy into it anymore.

*
Simple R*evolution
The muses, the smiling people around ~
If nobody's a Perfect Program then so am I.
How he wants the crutches of his five senses.
All of them together, enjoying Maximum Orgasm!
Rubbing, going mad with her tasty buds!
Making You into her Slave master.

*
STOP THINKING
Allow all the rational Madness
Let it be ~

Red & White Flags

Eternal Crusaders on the horizon ~
Inside the city gates, in your house!
Why wouldn't they want Revenge ~
when they blown his family to bits?
Ego, lust for POWER, 'Darth Vadar
lives in the US. Yoda lives in Russia'
Only nature can sort it out
Time can't be understood ~
Space is black always giving
birth to galaxies ~ SHIVA
has the Power to destroy the
Material World. KRISHNA
is the Spiritual Universe.
You wanna play God?
Maya enters your head
and she hypnotises you.
Drops of the Ocean ~
Zero point God Is Love.

*

Specs. Free

"I'll send the Limousine, shouldn't have done that!
'Shit goes on like that all the time ~
somewhere on the spinning Planet'
Cosmic Shamanic*The best Karma
Chains of Gold, born in a Penthouse
on Pacific Palisades! Be my guest.
Why beat around her bush?
All the hotels are booked up.
...... Lie a bit!

Deep Zen

"You can't conquer horse chestnuts
You can only roast them!"
The concept of being Free.
Pissed off I couldn't fulfill her dream.
Ok go and find a better one...
"Why should you have to go out
of your way to avoid anyone?"
Who has good Intuition ~
You're just putting about
the Love Energy

*

Too moody

They're all performers ~ too fluffy
they all wanna be Yoginis & DJs.
Up for a good time.
"What do you want
What can I do for you
What can you do for me?"

*

Star*gazer

That's what people used to do,
watch the stars*go by ~ Seeing ultra
violet patterns of sacred geometry
In the sky. Pure Sunshine into CBD.
What is this illusion of Freedom?

*

Secret

They know it ~
We don't know it....

Crazy Paving
Waving the Rebel flag ~ Outside the Asylum.
'If you're insane you don't know you're insane'
"I'm a Conscientious Objector
Rockin' in the Free World ~"
And it's the other way round!
Gain or lose with Ease ~
Fear into the system, disease.
Acting on the body and Mind.
Simply coming from the heart.
*The Miracle of Life * Flower*
with no mental-concept ~
of its conscious essence.

*

*Anonymous*Clicking*
Those people love their Pacific Ocean ~ Not anymore!
"A war in the name of Buddha, what the fuck!"
"I don't give a fuck about Fukushima Baba!"
"I Am Free Man Resonance"

*

*Synthetically*Wild Space*
'Drugs can be good for you'
The healing powers of LSD.
Nature's just Biochemical.
*A Wizard's*Alchemy chest.*
I remember that garden now ~
Cashing it in to Biological Capital.
'Photosynthesis ~ easiest conversion
of Sunlight into matter'

In the Illusion of Thinking
'The essence is eternal not in the words'
If you don't Identify with what's in your mind
It doesn't matter where you are.
Identifying with it, it is suffering ~ Breaking
the attachments, judgments and expectations.
Surrender consciously ~ experience what you are
inside is who you are.

*

Awareness & Consciousness
Legs spread apart an open invitation to fuck her!
State of compassion for those lost in the feelings
in their own minds ~ transcendence ~ otherwise ~
You see the insanity, look in yourself and forgive.
Accept people as Unconscious or it never works out.
Ego ~ you're doing it in your head to think about it.
It needs the mental reaction to feed its own Identity.
You can never know the truth, the whole truth, so help me

*

Greedy & Rich
Crazy World ~ they want to know everything!
Past & future ~ Mental Interference…
Tuning into the essence knowing
you are that Conscious Space ~
We're trapped in it*our own mind,
Your enemy, conflict in the duality.
Within you, accept your inner space ~
not outer space*Transmute consciousness.
Another separation another pain another
veiled threat, another heart breaking down.

<u>Affirmations</u>
"I like my Life ~"
I like my Freedom"
For sure ~ Giving up &
letting it happen naturally, consciously.
'Enlightened' ~ caught in this alphabet.
Wordless, I'm happy where I am.
I never said I believe in you…
Tantric is Love done with detachment,
freedom ~ your connection to others.
"I'd hate to die with ½ million quid in the bank."
LOVE is the answer ~
Vomiting on the way to the airport!
If you're serving people put a smile on your face.
Synchronistic Space ~ Giving out good energy.

*

<u>Coconut Power</u>
Have a 'Live Seed' Bank
Enjoying life's perfume ~
Not a GMO Concrete jungle
worshipping the golden cow
educating children about rats.
Really it's a Tree Not a palm or grass mate.
You are reflecting Nature in the Universal mirror.
Low caste raped by higher caste; Don't say a word or…
She'll suicide or they'll threaten to kill her whole family!
How is your psychology ~ 'Life is a dream pain is reality'
Death is holding on not going with ever changing Cosmic flow ~
Identifying with FORM, - Big block of thinking You already know!
Beam me up Vishnu!

You have to do it

If you start giving things will change ~
Can you give me LOVE? And it will be LOVE.
Don't wait for them to come to you.
Trusting in my inner self.
I don't have to Know and I'll
give you the right answer ~
True intelligence is beyond the mind.
Listen to it as it is ~ no identifying with it.
"I am angry" "What does it feel like… when
my attention goes into unconsciousness space?"
Identification with Ego created thoughts in my head.
Take an almond put it over your 3rd eye ~
Putting your tongue in the Soma.
"Oh, it's anger passing through ~"
In the eternal stillness

*

We are the fallen angel

Looking for a treasure that's already inside you ~
A mental abstraction that appears to be the Truth.
Believing in it when it's not even real!
They do know it but they're not conscious they know it.
Putting an Object there, the job of their doing.
We forget all the simple truths. 'To be or Not to be?'
It doesn't matter what you're doing you're in the being.
Accept it for what it is, couldn't be better ~ You're alive.

Sitting on your cushion
Smoking and meditation, that's the life!
"I found this old bottle of acid when
I was cleaning out the drawers ~"
They're products, Robots of the Control systems.
Relaxation is dreaming poetry in a Rose garden.
"He's lucky he's not in a sweatshop Baba!"
Chinadom ~ Needs rebalancing
*

Falling in Love
The thought of an emotion…
Making an assumption of what it is.
Try giving and letting it go ~
The Ego state wanting to own it
taking full possession as a right!
"I've got an exclusive on a grapefruit tree
which means I can eat all the fruit."
"Thank you very much"
*

In essence
Enthusiastic & Keen, putting the two together
"Keen doesn't make you smile like enthusiastic does."
Why f.....g Suffer Baba? "I keep this Mind-Space clear"
How do you wake people up?
Life wakes you up!
ID. with the eternal space inside you

<u>Lines of Coke*Uncovered</u>
'The Universe is CONSTANTLY CHANGING ~'
It's there to bring Illusions that's how they hide
Real truth, purpose is to brainwash the masses.
"When did you last see a chillum in Anjuna?"
Brainwashed believing in 72 voracious virgins, but
on Earth it's controlled they're not allowed free sex.
They also believe in the weekly female slave Market;
which is ordained so any act is possible in God's name!
Who's trying to eradicate the poor not poverty
And enslave the rest of us?
So is Heaven & Hell a Myth?
Govinda's super happy Gopis.
Let Krishna be your charioteer.
Always inside you 'Inner Peace'
'Only if you're part of it ~
then it can be part of you.'
We Are the Creators.

*

<u>LOVE</u>
Deep down underwater ~
Coming up for air together.
On different trajectories….
Find the place where there's
no right or wrong narcosis.
Come and meet me there.

Too much Regime

Hash, Cocaine, smack, ketamine, changa, meow,
crack not there to make the people thinking!
Psychedelic T shirts, 'You're too colourful!'
You can get locked up for having a hair out
of your headscarf, reciting poems in Riyadh.
Head chopped off for whistling at her arse.
Adam & Lilith were equal, she liked to party
on the coast with the Lesbians and Demons.
Adam was gutted so God made gorgeous Eve
out of mud & a rib to keep him happy ~ Women
got no rights there not even a Provisional License.

*

Kali's Seduction

Stretching her soft orchid velvet lips over his pumping cock!
The tongue swallowing a fat line; Ready for the meat!
'Don't make her feel like a guest, make her feel at home'
Keep the 'New Karma Sutra' on your bedside table.
Energy of Planet Venus living in the Celestial sky.
Energy of the Goddess affecting the Moon's waters.
Caught in the spinning emotional patterns... STOP!
Creating Maya's Time-machine Illusions. STOP IT-
It loses all Forms disintegrating into Cosmic Space.
When it transcends Earth, sees all God's as Earth's Gods.
'Shiva is the only one not born, no birth so he doesn't die'
Sucking up & down a spiral Vortex ~ Life is smiling at you.

<u>Coming from the heart</u>

Bless her every day because one day you'll go away ~
Doing as you please right now, not in a future or a past.
The Priests who obey the Government, who'll hang you!
Blame game of sex, women, snakes, the mad illuminated,
other schools of thought. 'Thou shalt not sit in judgment'
God made the apple how can it be evil? Ask yurself mate
A conditioned mind not wanting the primordial of fucks!
A fuck through that only will life continue ~ not any taboo.
"You want that big cock to fuck my pussy?"
"They're not Bombing anyone
they're just enjoying a fuck!"

*

<u>P O S S E S S I O N*P O S S E S S E D</u>
"He's my bird, I can do whatever I f..... want!"
Why not let the bird decide what it wants for living
its own natural life ~ Peacefully or as a predator?
Outside the Box ~ Do Not Think!
And we've all been here since the beginning.
Energetic Love-making, call me when you feel like it.
She's a welder ~ An artist in metal, a conscious chemical reaction.
Oxytocin's*2nd cuming wrapped in white light*I like Visuals.
Once you get out of the mental grip ~ we can enjoy this trip.
Nature sends you more making you stronger.
Higher consciousness otherwise you'll perish.
'One has to go where one has to go'
"She's not your slave mate"

Exe*cutting*Gene*side
"If God didn't want us to eat animals
he wouldn't have made them out of meat!"
Charged with Apostasy and abandoning one's faith.
Another Poet sentenced to death for blasphemy.
Beheading, they say he said things against God.
How about opening the body to the golden light?
Why aren't you putting sanctions
on the countries buying ISIS oil?
Why are you destroying millions
of innocent people? Really Why?
*

Ex O Set
The Headlock to Heaven!
"Don't lock onto her eyes."
More Beauty and a Beast!
Love straight from Holland!
"You can't let go of something
if you don't know what it is"
*

Nose Ring
'An infusion of Queen Anne's Lace seeds, the wild
progenitor of our cultivated 'carrot' (Celtic, 'Red')'
Take any pressure out ~
Take any expectation out!
She should just relax.
Listen to her body ~
Welcome a birthing

Red Ganesha by the Door
"Don't believe anything I say go out and do it yourself."
Everything he said was Gold. 'Pain is clinging on!'
Born in the Kali dimension of desiring Maya.
An affliction not always been a good Buddhist.
That damn mosquito, free to make my own choice.
Wants everyone thinking of their root chakra forever!
"There's this energy...."
"Shut the fuck up!"

*

More precious than Gold
Beyond the mental act of materialisation,
I would stand naked in that dimension.
*Flowers don't have brains*like us*
chemicals attracting natural Procreators.
Enjoying floral bliss ~ It's a mystery to a lot of people.
Space and nature it's all in your head.
One of the biggest lies not told....
Seeing the Sun*Moon not seeing the Space
holding it all together ~ Seeking something more.
Reality of a picture/puzzle it's another dimension.
Understanding the Spirit.

*

Bail
They'll take Visa in Jail!
'They can't lock you up ~
when you are Free Inside'

<u>DESIROUS</u>

'Deja Vu' a great movie.... Classic.
'The obstacle is the path' ~ Zen proverb.
'Meditation ~ Quieting the Mind, being Stillness'
Shows you no deception from this clear space.
A thought can make you laugh or cry.
'Is it, was it, says it is?'
In the intellectual*flesh plane.
Coming out into the Silence of the light
All things bright ~ 'It is what is ultimately'

*

<u>Panic Attacks in Pylon City</u>
'If you're working you feel you're being used'
Like the living death, delirium ~
Shocks & traumas of fright, full of fear.
Going in the sea up to her ankles...
Seduced one year by the old apple tree"
"OK everyone stash your stuff!"
1968 Revolution, people opening windows onto a Summer of Love.
George Orwell the prophet of a subliminally controlled political world.
From a system of mass conditioning, Manipulation being manifested
as only Fear and desire of the unreal Ego persona, denying life,
looking for tomorrow's reward when it doesn't exist ~ only in the Now!
Being a vagabond in Paris with an inspirational poet; Leonard Cohen's
"And Suzanne takes you down to her place near the river ~
She feeds you tea and oranges that come all the way from China
And you touch her perfect body with your mind ~

That's an Old Tree
'God delusional' stuff! Pacifying some Insane Deity!
Holy Massacring of 100,000 buffalo in Nepal!
"In Italy you're not allowed to live in a tent in your garden."
Lighting a chillum ~ take off and fly... Forget the Past!
When the 'I Am' is talking, not Jesus just a name'
Waves of Buddha nature ~ Party On!

*

Bio*Queen*Bee*Your Answer
'Investing in Alternative energy
Protecting Life Not Gold.'
The Sub-conscious Mind ~
taking over the dreamtime.
songs of Paradise on Earth.

*

F.... No Choice 'Cold Pussy!'
Unconscious super Ignorant cruel, painful withdrawal.
Deep Spiritual extraction from freezin' Self-extinction
of a Love Addiction cutting me off at the balls ~
At some point in infinite time * Soul*free Space

*

Cosmic Logic Groove
"I have no Brand name burnt into me ~"
Light is Might * May the Brightness Prevail
A Killer, seeing your Ex-wife with someone else!
All perception ~ realising how precious a breath is.
The simplicity of just breathing in the presence ~
'You can't know what you are because you are it'
Enlightening darkness let the Innocent Angels fly free.
Love * Light Happiness & Peace, blessings for all of us.

Kebabs are Cordon Bleu in Wales
They all want stuff, shampoos to champagne.
'What's the point of not being friendly?'
Why waste your time thinking about it?
Realize your own delusions see them dissolve.
It's inevitable it will happen ~ Anything, Snake bight,
shark attacks by the NSA; cluster bombs in your school!
Sadhus who've renounced the world now need an ID card!
Can't buy Karma cleaner putting all you got in the church plate.
What seeds you planting for your sweet mango tree garden mate?
Giving money to the Church authority out of fear of more damnation!
Signor Escobar put his treasure in the Vatican Bank, c/o Bogota.
He designed and built his own jail with guards, on top of a hill.

*

You become Poetic
"I believe in You." "I don't believe You." Anymore, too much pain!
Depends how real it is ~ Samson & Delilah at the Eden spa.
It's a commercial Planet ~ should have charged him for it!
Sprouting the seeds of deception and devotion. You'll never
get hurt swimming with Romantics in the Sea of Possession?
Deceitful ~ "Don't expect Love that's the biggest Fuck-up!"
All your dreams shattered, emotional state haywire! Lamp
of Life, offerings of flowers, do the mantras get siddhis
The body is your Temple of purities, then you're a Yogi.
Travelling with Space chicks to the far side of the Moon.
Models don't come free!

Nisargadatta Maharaj
'Spiritual maturity is being ready to let go everything ~ Giving
up is a first step, but real giving-up is the insight that there's
nothing to be given up, since nothing is your property.'

*

Dissonant Separation
Life is vibration ~ sound, colour, everything
Achieving resonance vibrating at the same rate
Amplitude ~ power of each wave magnetized
Tick tocking at the same time
You can be the Lover and make your own Magic!
You're the centre of the wheel*watching it spinning around.

*

Earthing*Zeitgeist
Feeling it with all our Attention, senses not thinking,
LIVE + going through your body into the ground.
"Everybody's dealin' with different stuff."
Taught to me by an ancient DMT plant.
Touching Life energy going into the Earth.

*

PERFECT DESIRE'S ALLOWANCE
'There was/is an Angel by my side ~'
Perfect moments of life * Cosmic pilgrimages.
Embracing your being ~ feeling you deep inside me.
Our waves flowing together ~ through Oceanic Space
"Kali Yuga only cash will work!"
Not counting your mala standing on your head.
"I am not in a fuckin' Zoo"

<u>They allowed the fugitive to leave</u>
Countering the spin of the Media Machine
Cancelled his passport – to Expel him back...
The USA Prisoner transportation plane on standby.
A former CIA Rendition monster prepared to take off.
Who'd like a job with the Russian Intelligence Service?
Staking her entire life on it, Terminal F; kept them in a transit
Zone. Needs protection not a prison cell, denied asylum in all of
Puppet Europe's false democracies! Disinformation of a diversion,
Alienated the Eagle all over the world. A brilliant escape strategy.
False flag ~ Not escorted with President Morales to casa Bolivia.
No safe passage to Latin America, US criminals forcing down
a decoy jet! The Fascists have cancelled all diplomacy
and skyjacked a Head of state, confirmed with the NSA!

*

<u>Open*Knowledge</u>
'Please note: Smashwords ebooks are licensed for YOUR
enjoyment ONLY.' Thank you for that! Loving what is *
*'Savage aborigines' not wild but **FREE**; One word can cast*
a Magic spell creating y/our mass Perceptions via our filters!
Instantaneous brainwashing focusing on the ultimate illusion.
It's not the invisible Man but the Elephant is crying in the room!
Happy Space*Man. I hear the monks chanting from the Gompa.
Sabda (sacred sound) is powerful Invoking attributes of the Spirit
Goddess, her devotional Love. She occupies all my chakras ~
Timeless essence her Mons Veneris dancing within my Pleiadian stars

SUPRA*MAYA
We all got it in us ~
different light frequencies, bandwidth.
Darkness is coming out the cupboard!
The Consensus believes in their Programming.
Oh yeah let's have some more of that, acceptance!
'Standing by the road & a bus hits you; They blame you!'
"Understanding I'm living the life I'm meant to live"
Some don't have a choice, majority don't Understand.
*"I'm doing what I want, **FREELY** ~ It's Why 'I' exist!"*
"The music will even bring me a girlfriend ~"
A loving, uncomplicated, devoted Parvati.

*

If someone owed me $232 billion Obviously it's not gonna be easy to get it back but then I don't believe it's time for a lecture on Democracy! Pay your debts like the rest of us are obliged to do then we can all have an ouzo at the shack on the beach and or find the people who ripped you off. Where'd the money go in the first place? Ask at the empty hole in the Wall street…

*

Blissful Live
"Up to your neck in shit!"
Easy to do ~ come off the rails!
All those Ego lessons ~
Are there for us to learn…
Create the Love Vibration
Finding the Spirit

On Monsoon flooding

Nepal tent city, aftermath of the 2015 Earthquake.
The Government of Nepal has the resources, the IMF has
resources as shown by the bailouts of Greece etc. This is at least a
massive (tragic) disappointment! WTF. is up with this greedy World?
Are the Powers that be so inhuman when with some consciousness ~
this could be changed. But not one house built after six months! Why?
Where is the leadership? The Reporting is an indictment of Corruption,
of Society/Authority, those who abrogated the Power have the means
but are as usual so pathetically inept!

*

Hardcore Chilly

Brainwashed, we all got a heart, no not everybody!
"Mind is a phantom it will go to the grave with you"
They're special puppets because bigger demons take the power.
Mind's function is to keep you entrapped in this mental Universe.
You are just You, no knowledge will change that spiritual act.
That's why everyone has a brain * 7 billion + versions of us.
Everything just comes and goes ~ 38 kilos and ringing wet!

*

Win

A cigarette factory next to a nuclear waste dump in China!
There's a lot of cowboys in England; Renowned for it...
Humble Shiva, he's a detached Yogi not an Emperor.
He's not wasting his time meditating on us ~
Without Shakti nothing would exist materially having
no knowledge about the qualities of God's Forms.
Forget the body & Mind ~ dancing inside right now!

PLEIADES*POP

_Somehow to rationalise these stark extremes * of the concept
of a dualistic – Conditioned-mind makes Sense and we react
accordingly however there is a Buddhist perspective whereby
'Anicca' is Realisation that these concepts are only formulations
of our own Ego which is the driving force of Mental formations ~
based on being Attached to the manifestation from which it derives
its energy ~ However by being aware of this process of the Ego*
*Universe we can at some point be detached from it and accept
whatever happens to happen and to respond by knowing it is Not
Personal. This allows for nature to exist through its essence in our
heart in an ever-changing holistic, dynamic, synergetic synchronistic
being here now vibe ~_

*

'LIVE AND LET LIVE'

_ELIMINATE*ILLUMINATE * Another CrISIS of Consciousness.
Can't recognise our True Nature in everyone and in All things >
(Objects/Forms).That we all are essentially of the same SPACE
'Do unto others as you will have done unto yourself'_
'Live simply so that others may simply live'
_The war instigated on Vietnam and admitted in US Government
records was a complete fabrication and a lie, a Crime Against
Humanity and Genocide! Why is this still allowed to happen?
'Times' –'Today the USA has 5% of the world's population but
also they have 25% of the world's prison population more than
Stalin had at the height of his dictatorship.' "There's nothing ~
more exhilarating & seductive than a change in consciousness"
Let all beings be free ~ to 'Make Love Not War Consciousness'_

Einstein's View

'Insanity is doing the same thing over and
over again and expecting different results'
"A human being is part of a whole, called by us
the Universe, a part limited in time and space ~
'He experiences himself, his thoughts and feelings ~
as something separated from the rest - a kind of optical
delusion of his consciousness.' This delusion is a prison
made for us, restricting us to our personal desires and to
affection for a few persons nearest us. Our task must be to
free ourselves from this prison by widening our circles of
compassion to embrace all living creatures and
the whole of nature in its beauty."
*

Different Force Fields which are not y/our Infinite Self
I know the vampire story we just have to somehow BE ~
the Vampire slayer with love in the heart. It's a fucked up
World in many ways and miscommunication with a loved one
is very tough and yet so common. It will make you an Angel
if you can survive! It seems to me somehow we
have to step back because of OUR own feelings***
An inner sense of joy, insight, purpose and inspiration.
I've been floating in a lake of quiet depression for awhile
but you KNOW it's NOT true and we have more to aspire to
in this marvelous life***Go for it Baba be the heroic knight
battling dark forces**Do what YOU NEED to maintain
your *LIGHT & PEACE* of brilliant im/perfect humanity.

What we're fed
I wasn't thinking about it ~ I was just a dolphin.
A Lake of Light ~ Waves coming through Crystals.
Broken legs, Farmed chickens, the Poisoned Apple.
'No such thing as FREE WILL, all is so manipulated!'
The women getting raped now are by the Police!
Paedo Pan, Selfie Sufi & Pikey Sthani's profiles.
What's Awareness gotta do with it?
Everybody should STOP Eating meat
RIGHT NOW!

*

Cheap Buzz
Some Sanity in an Insane World.
Just breathe it in ~ each to their own
Beyond the 5 senses ~ You bring in the 6th sense!
Seeing into nature's male wave ~ female wave
Complimentary

*

Awareness*Mirroring
'Love is what you're born with
Fear is what you Learn'
The Fear of All My Fears!
Livin' off the grid, off the radar.
Sometime she's gonna have to pull out her Magic wand!
An inter-dimensional Robin flyin' beside a Kailash Moon.
You're looking for what you are ~ already!
Embrace the Present ~ being here now
Why do I need to do yoga to breathe ~
I am already breathing ~ sitting on a rainbow..

Quantum*Energy
Dimensionless Space ~ timeless waves
Observations are Limiting things. Labeling it ~
Kierkegaard ~ 'If you name something we negate it by limiting it
so negating all other things I could be creating at the same time.'
Embedded in the Matrix*TIME*SPACE*Fractal's chaotic mind defines
Patterns as things. To comprehend a fractal with the senses is to limit its
movement in order to Recognise a THING, to hold its pattern in our Mind.

*

Drone Rules
Hacked again by a Paranoid Smurf in a mask ~
Android smart cells much too tempting to ignore.
Ask at Digital Weapons, Intelligence & Espionage.
Secretly taking over the Network service providers.
"They really want to own you" We've come to the end.
"Fair enough if someone's gonna kill you,
You gotta fight back ask any Palestinian!"

*

Dawn Chorus' Beat
"Are you in the Mudra for Love?"
'Spontaneous' ~ that's a good word & 'Economic War'?
More biomass, Hemp than they know what to do with!
Playing tones in the garden of delights
The right vibrational frequency ~
Playing fecund resonances back to them
for a longer, juicier Stigmata.

Martial State v Nature
'They weren't Wild they were just Free ~'
Changing our Perceptions of Ourselves.
No Freedom ~ no emotional Magic.
"The lights might not come on again!"
"Stay at home or you'll be shot dead!"
New Speed Dictionary, def. 'Denatured'
Live essence in all of us ~ Who are you?
The Supernatural driver written into Crystal
tablets of Holographicity floating in the sky.
Now ~ seeing the Universe in 'Real Time'
As a data hybrid sharing off-World Info-Intel.
Then there'll be the War on Aliens!
'I Love these Angels coming down'
*

Crystal Planet Amsterdam
"You're living in the past" "Oh no!"
Again & again & again and it's Not nice.
Only holding on to painful memories ~
Memories of betrayal, anger and hate.
Family, real family of your Soul mate ~
Sunlight strokes the Mons Pubis of Venus.
"Fuck man where's my gun?"
Where's the Coral reef?
Reality ~ Life's a Biche

<u>Looking into her eyes</u>
"Heroin has more ~ absence of Sensation.
Drop the dialectic line or you're tied to it!
The habit's you creating super highways of sad thoughts.
That's how I got out of it, think of something Happy ~
In yourself, accelerating through rainbows changing.
If you don't toe the line victim, don't hate anyone.
I looked at it from a multi*dimensional perspective,
rewiring my whole head, letting yourself feel good.
'War on drugs' is proven nonsense try some Vipassana.
The way you see you're in/out of Control, not depressed!
You are messing up the air fire water earth deliberately!
Gone, seeing the illusion for what it is in the light.
Good people energy, I love that they're happy ~
What you get conned into; "I got 38 qualifying years!"
They're warming up the Blue beam lasers for a big show.
Stoned enough, Save a Planet, 'I'm going to grow wings'
*

<u>"I keep my mind empty"</u>
If it's full of stuff that's already happened that's a drag
I don't wanna keep those things on my mind, 100%!
"Why not have a thought that makes you smile ~"
Look in the mirror after a week, tell me what you see.
It could be a golden Paradis*it could be full of tragedy!
I did it once for my own self-destruction.
"I flew out of it, worked it out for myself,
had no choice, had to."

MAYA * MATRIXICAL

We make it Real * Super Yogis.
It's all about Sublime Empathy.
Why do you have to believe it?
A doubt, a fear, a blockage, pain.
Caught in the matter of atoms & molecules.
'Looking for the soul when you are the soul'
How many times do you want to go through that?
It's endless & an Amazing Illusion
More books, more knowledge, more details
Going on and on ~
The Power in chanting Mantras
The Universe is constantly changing
In Infinite Space ~ Bhakti devotion.
More than you can ever think of.
Inner supernatural entering you
And that's just the beginning.
Natural ~ You're breathing
Whether focused or not.
Then you'll get a spiritual experience
And wonder why you wasted your life.
OM NAMAH SHIVAYA

*

Oceanic
"The more psychedelics you use ~
the less meditation you need to do"

Kali Yuga

"I guess it's my fault for thinking that shit should work"
English Privateer's on-going Royal charter to Invade!
'The only war now is for Global NWO Conquest.
Elite fighting for their survival, DNA program!'
"In a time of Universal deceit telling the truth
*is a revolutionary act" * George Orwell.*
"I don't wanna be a Nazi, I Know that!"

*

On the Planet

Making the name 'Pacifist' into a dirty word!
"Scientists say man is responsible for making everything"
When we realise the Power
of Gaia, the Divine, Cosmic God, they all kneel.
Don't ask me, "I'm ok with that now ~
Nobody knows!

*

Drop*Out

"Real food that's come out of the ground"
Levitated out of the System...
All based on an idea of You and Me ~
And our extended family living in the canopy.
Because Me doesn't last very long ~ What's that about?
Back to square one ~ The Image, Perception.
"Oh, I had a Spiritual experience"
"They won't talk to you again!"
The Brightest and the dumbest of them all.
'IT'S THE MATRIX STUPID!'
Stingray couriers to Venus' smoldering Starlets

<u>Rule</u>
DIVIDING
&
CONQUERING
ALL of YOU/US
*

<u>Love</u>
Is the feeling ~
we share together.
Kali killed my Ego.
Heart on fire
Asking for that Ultimate high.
Be here now Baba
Enjoy the moment*sans drame
*

<u>Motivated*Animated</u>
I'm Free to choose whatever I want
but it makes me laugh when it happens.
That's what you want ~ Out in the Open
Otherwise you're playing games of Tiddlywinks!
Infatuation full on, no minding your own business.
Getting on with it and for a moment someone gives you
T O T A L   F U L F I L L M E N T
Non*Perception when you've no way of lookin at it.
You are it ~ Deep inside Consciousness.
I Am deep Space ~ Awareness of your essence
'There's a rainbow inside your head ~ just groove on it.'

<u>*Super soul where yu trippin?*</u>
Dancing in another dimension ~
He's dancing in everyone with everyone.
They want more money, 'Gandhi not Shanti'
The whole nation's running after it!
"What the hell, what the fuck ~ Google it!"
How to fill all your cushions with diamonds.
Try living in a cave with a sofa full of gold.
Jetting to it ~ just another one of your movies.
The tree talks to them ~ "Use us!" it says.
*

<u>*Smoking Molten Heat*</u>
'Humans following One Robot!'
It's a crime to run out of money.
"That's my ticket back to Babylon!"
"They're lookin' at us like Junkies!"
"It must be an amazing sight seeing
someone we know go up in flames!"
"They got the Spirit Power Baba"
*

<u>*Not Scared*</u>
'Chillums not around ~ Beer bottles everywhere!'
What we need, fresh out the shower.
Street kids don't live for tomorrow ~
& he bought the biggest dog in the world. Why?
'If you don't feel it how can you believe in it?'
"Feeling is everything"

<u>Corporate*Networking*Cyber Police.</u>
Graduated cum-laude from Saturnalia.
'Have a nice day; You'll really Love this!'
Advertising on Billboards outside your house!
Negativity it sticks to you like a bus going
round the corner, spaying you with shit!
This stuff is defining y/our reality; All bollocks!
"How can it be a crime to tell the Truth? Basics.
How can it be illegal to help set a Slave free
from the herd going to market?"

*

<u>Fractal * Moments</u>
That girl ~ Total Spirit
She could have been a hippie on the beach
with energetically inspired sky blue eyes ~
Time flies.

*

<u>To Be King of Telepathy</u>
Moving in & out of Time*Space ~
Created another Heavenly Planet.
Jingling Apsaras came down to Earth
dancing for his supreme delight.
Loving the 7 constellations.
"Go break his meditation!"
Forever in heaven when you
get your real dose of DMT!

King is second to God!
He cheated with Magic dice.
She was a Krishna devotee ~
Where is the original Mahabharata now?
Sanskrit, 'Swastika' ~ 'The Wheel of Time'
Hoping to go back to Aryan's Golden India.
Another Mythology, full of misunderstanding!
"I don't hate you, you can hate yourself if you wish'

*

Virtually*Maya
'SHE'S FUCKED IT OFF - IT DOESN'T WORK!'
Teaching to merge back into your identity.
Way of explaining through FORM.
It's just another Pipe-dream!
Lot of Painters and decorators in Prison.
Lotta Possession * no Creativity ~
The only one not dragged into the Mire
always on Cosmic meditation, being centered.
He's the golden light, she's his beloved devotee.
'Reflecting the light in the truth of their spiritual nature'

*

Can you do that?
"Leave Heaven what can you do there?"
Unselfish merging back to Godhead.
More important than the temporary
Orbiting Planets of Paradise
'When you're in it ~ it's Real'

<u>Just a Dream</u>
The day you drop the 'I Am'
the Universe disappears like a speck of dust.
Back to Supreme Consciousness.
Out of the clutches of Maya ~
You never were Sunny Jetsun.
Endless Work, that's another Maya.
All memories ~ where did it come from?
You're not that dream.

*

<u>Detoxed Hi-Tech Trance</u>
At the Speed of Light ~186,000 miles per second.
Eight minutes to arrive here from the Sun's rays.
"This water is Alive* with Life*energy particles"
You're another Happy customer
Needs a complete strip down...
Say YES to Reality
Say YES to Beauty
from the land of Promises.

*

<u>Conscious Atoms*Krishna's Moons</u>
"The Bible is a good book to civilise the Barbarians"
Yogis doing meditation for eons to know the Truth.
If the chemistry is right she'll feel a blessing ~
from the Solar dynasty and send it straight to you.
All the plants, animals & stones, everything's moving ~
Outer Space * Cosmic aliens more powerful than Earthlings.

God Loves You
Lotus ponds lost in the catacombs of Roman Gods' minds...
Alive Planetary Consciousness beyond our comprehension....
Coming in interstellar flying chariots from blue Star galaxies.
Shiva consciousness beyond the effects of the full Moon.
Trouble starts with materialism ~ conquered their natural life!
'He's giving you Heaven on Earth'

*

Human beings are defined by their feelings*for each other
Making another DIY. extension to my Asylum ~
Why aren't all poor people living in hammocks?
Need a Government with a sunshine perception!
"I don't need to read a book to tell me right from wrong"
'The only way to deal with an unfree world is to become so
Absolutely Free that your very existence is an act of Rebellion.
A. Camus…. Nothing to do ~ being the happiest man in the World.
Depleted uranium 238, bullets, radiation half-life of 4,468 billion years!
Bombed the whole area with armor piercing white phosphor artillery!'
You'll wake up with Fallujah defects and poisoning on your burnt body.
It's never in the press, in the media; No Wikileaks to keep them honest.
'I believe the people with all the money in the world run the big Diorama.
know the puppet show, green screen, swings, balances, horror & Love

*

Getting Rid of a Load of Shit
"This is just beautiful beyond belief!"
"The more you see the more it unfolds"
Focusing on the delicate bliss ~ healing.
At a Psychedelic * Entheogenic Retreat.
Be your own Satguru mate ~ when you get that feelin'

Mother's Compassion
'He's fucked it off again ~ it doesn't work!'
No one can leave the Universal ~
without getting permission from Kali.
Poisonous Cobra's ~ Man's False Ego.
Mastering his Tiger passion, it senses him.
Transcend all the dreams of Heaven and Hell.
Forgiveness, empathy, humbleness you're a yogi.
Cosmic Love * Shiva Consciousness of the whole
from Durga to a blade of grass to a glowing star.

*

Simple Advice
You can't hypnotise him anymore, he's full!
Been in the matrix years ago ~ now let it go
"I don't believe in anything anymore"
Once you climb through the scenery.
'Moved on, happy, hope you are too'
You always hear about the enslaved
not the Free wo/man.

*

'It will be whatever it is'
All Neo-Conceptualising, the Mind ~ Things named...
Perceived patterns, poetic weaves of an onlooker.
"Can't I enjoy it when I'm not with what I love?"
'Hatred doesn't cease by hatred, hatred ceases by Love'
Dhammapada*AS I AM*
Life is a reflection of Light

Bag of Bush
Most people have their heads stuck up their root chakras!
You either go up or you go down ~
Here on time
*

*Cyber*Baba*
"The Injuns are coming!"
Floating around Anjuna battered!
Expressing a positive direction ~
Fully naked inside her ~ I fuckin' love it!
It's hard to say NO, I'm enjoying it, I like it.
Not many on it and too many not on it!
'100% dependent unless it's running wild'
Gotta stop it from doing what it's doing…
A little river in India that's what you want Baba.
Done all the Yoga, had all the self-realisation
been with all the gurus ~ Beautiful not horrible.
*

Thanks to Everyone
People are being slaughtered…
& the sweet tenderness of that kiss!
Buildings collapsing on top of you,
You're still alive!
The Sun will shine again

<u>The Kiss in Slaughterhouse 6 ~ It's Love</u>
There's something Spiritual beyond the violent ignorance ~
"My happiness is not determined by what's going on outside but inside
Not by my environment ~ I can be happy everywhere. "It's all talk!"
"I Am a Free radical*electron surfing through Cosmic consciousness"

*

<u>Krishna said "let it go ~</u>
Super confidence ~ the innocence of a child.
'Guilty' comes from Babylon, Corporate Slavery!
You didn't choose your name did you? Birth Cert. Fraud.
It didn't happen to you, it just happened, that's it!
"What we can see, observe cannot be us,
Because I AM the one seeing it.

*

<u>A Sacred Charisma</u>
I can be anywhere ~ I don't care
Happy Inside Myself
'There are good things everywhere'
'There are bad things everywhere'
Doesn't matter about the environment
or where you are ~ Keep it Real.
Finding that place of harmony

*

<u>Finance is the Devil</u>
'Freedom is another illusion'
Flashback, outside the Prison, FREE!
Threw me out on Christmas eve, concept.
On X factor the Prison's male carol singers.
A giant decorated Christmas tree in the yard.

Arrest the Judge
If you have no compassion
You are not a feeling human...
Even animals have compassion ~
They're neither animal or human!
Computers slowly formatting our brains,
connecting our Minds to the MATRIX ~
We're not seeing it ~ focusing on yourself.
'The Real thing is Feeling'
I AM CONSCIOUS
*

Karma Circus
Ordering Elephants and Tigers in a Germanic accent!
Making a spiritual investigation at the Dragon Dolmen.
A long memory of massacres ask any Lakota Sioux ~
"Don't want any more F..... PAIN"
That's what Gotama said before he became enlightened!
What's going on Inside!
*

On/Off
Signals to your main-frame membrane.
The Nucleus is the brain of the cell ~
DNA in every fractal of the hologram.
Heart & Mind ~ it's processing all over time & space.
Tricking your Mind and skin's chemical sensations...
Reading the illusion, knowing what you were thinking.
Seeing the difference between trust/not trusting your feelings.
Going down into the DNA; lining up proteins of your Karma ~
We are the most complexity of life.

<u>Controlling Genes</u>
Everything is in us
We have tails, gills beaks claws and feathers
for when nature needs to transmute evolution...
Another mythological culture coming out the slime.
Flooded Earth, my girlfriend turning into a mermaid.
Our brain conjuring up a pre cognisance
Your body's reading the environment...
We'd be absolutely full of joy.
'We are absolutely Perfect'

*

<u>This is the Truth</u>
When you were a kid and did something wrong
You got smacked, locked you in your room alone.
All so familiar, sitting on a hard bed with no dinner.
I remember this

*

<u>Priceless Release</u>
"You never laugh like that outside Prison!"
Little treats that make you Happy ~
"saved the jam with some hot tea..."
Walkin' across the wing you heard him scream!
They don't give a shit!

*

<u>Flight or Fight</u>
Your body's in the real world ~
Conscious of every chemical around you
Cells and nerves scanning and reacting ~
Doing other things after making your mind up.
There's a reason why we get animated ~ to live in the now

It's a Great Place

'It's all a dream and I'll be living the dream'
He's had a grin on his face for two years...
Everywhere she went was the wrong place.
Angkor Wat is nice, ended up with a black dick!
The only thing they were talkin' about...
Alcohol, pussy and crystal meth!
No paranoia from his Ice dealer.
A scary twinkle in her eye.

*

Fr. 'Cash'

Straight to your face, looking into your eyes.
Matrix metaphor for what's happening ~
looking like the truth ~ dreaming their life in fact.
Crossing on theta waves in a hand-made cocoon.
Power of Pan, frolicking in Magical Consciousness.
Disconnected his real body out of the Miasma.
You Realise you're looking from the Inside out ~
Realising the transition. Take a Red pill, WAKE UP!
How you were so much in the delusion.
Living in an Illusion, I need a Ganesh T shirt.
Real thing is feeling*feeling*feeling

*

Smoking Mirrors

"If you stick your nose in shit ~
that's where the smell comes from."
"You're taking the piss!"
Nature is being snatched from us!
We are being programmed to lead an artificial,
Unnatural life

Negative-they're not Human
Pain let it be ~ it will pass....
It's in the processing of another moment ~
They want to break Reality! Split it into pieces of Infinity ~
Keeping you used to living under surveillance Mr Orwell.
Mind controlled programming from your HD. Plasma TV.
'Television Is Not the Truth, lying like hell making illusions!'
'The Tube is Not Reality mate' ~ don't be another maniac!
'Who Controls the cameras? TURN THEM OFF!'
'Paying them to turn you into a Slave'
Dictators telling you how to live.

*

Clever Hooks
Getting them to kneel at your Altar's feet.
People will pay you a fortune for the biggest distraction!
'We're more than we can think...'
'Claiming your natural freedom to Party ~'
Living by what you feel is right for yourself
'I Am.' Who Am I? I am nature changing infinitely.

*

Why Are You Alive?
Being in black space and I couldn't move ~
"I feel like I'm living in a Bladerunner movie"
Over there you can take your pick and have a laugh.
Pussy with a mind of its own and no extra headaches.
"I wanna have a Happy End Please dear"
Being nice with no limits as long as you can,
while they nail your balls to the wooden cross!
'Forgive them they don't know what they're f.... doin!'
'Beauty is in the eye of the beholder' ~ of course

Ma Motto
Be here now ~
What was it?
"I've forgotten what it was"
"Good evening officer..."
"I don't want any hassle"
It's about profits, making more money,
about exploiting the life-time of others.

*

Long Live the Poets
Worry about a Government telling you to worry 'bout Moslems!
"Do what you're told or we'll chop your hands off!"
Rounded up under Sharia law, this doesn't look good!
Indians love cricket.
That's what I think.

*

Happy Days
Our very own Cambodian stallion!
We got 'em all....
For those who would like the best sunrise ~
For that psychedelic sheep in the family
Taking you down deep into the Ocean ~ Space-Force.
Tantric beach-boy Baba taking you for an aerobics flight
with a happy naked landing; Kamadev he's up all night.
"Don't make me out to be a twat!"

Space-out
The Palace, top floor, hangin' over the balcony!
FEEL*********FREE********Are you gonna get*
what you want in the Andaman Islands?
What I need is a Mongolian beauty in a string bikini.
"I'll ordain that one for the Friday female slave market"
Would you want a slave Baba for Free?
Begging for it ~ Check it out!
*

Show us your diamonds
"I'll have to dive in and try to catch it in a plastic bag ~
"We all gotta get together and take the Top off the Pyramid"
The Gold always gets nicked first. Who's still got any sympathy?
'Accepting reality or Pain & Suffering!' They do kill people for sure!
"We promise you a Happy ending where the customer always comes first"
*

Jerusalem in bits
'jus primae noctis' vassal fundamentals ~ Neo feudalism!
'Opportunity Baba' 'Droit du Seigneur' taking everything as they do!
Everyone wants to be in Vogue; You never know what will happen.
Take a picture with a hippy ~ You want the best.
*

Gravitational Pull
Transcending beyond the 3rd dimension
On an elemental waterbed ~ Released to go
Consciousness is slowed down to light ~
light Ozone layer is slowed down to Matter.
'The Ramblings of a Mad Man' ~ "I like it!

Observer of the Cosmos
Meditation ~ Self-medicating in sweaty Cambodia.
They lost their connection to life, now just numbers.
Corporate legalised fraud by any other name!
'What we truly are rather than a lot of thoughts.'
Drones & robots developed to pollinate flowers ~
Whatever happened to the Birds and the Bees?
'They don't recognise the Coconut tree as a tree here!'
Anyone can chop them down and make into Fenni...
'Recognising all life form has the same equality'

*

Evil Genius
Build expensive things and blow them up!
Build expensive things and blow them up!
Build expensive things and blow them up!
It's like Robin Hood under the Oppressor
Cutting all the flowers

*

Kambo*Detoxin
What's it release you of? Everything!
Life flowing without being in the Mind ~
Super charged blood, reactions, wiping all that stuff off...
Anything conditioning you into holding you in that gravity?
Gotta ride that wave ~ "it's a long way to Tripperary...."
Get with it as soon as you can.
'Free for All'

A Great Start
War and murder on every corner ~
A Patriot missile going right, left, straight, right turn!
Not clever at all, you're still killing people!
"The next revolution of human beings will be the one
that can live in Peace and harmony with nature"
Responding in the moment rather than expectations.
GMO. Supermarket food with no Prana ~ no Life force...
"We are all Consciousness consuming Consciousness"
"It is better to eat an animal with Mindfulness than consume
vegetables without thought"

*

Ephemeral
What is Real? Magical Love.....
'It must be the most famous kiss in the world.'
There are many different kisses ~
they're never the same.
Gonna have to go and find a Temple..
Find the Temple dancers in a whirl ~
Take some Tulsi Baba ~ It was doin' it by Itself

*

& All things bright
'Let the Light of Love break the chains'
May you live in the Light and Love and may it
shine out from your hearts for all to feel this
undeniable, true quality of your Compassion ~
Sharing in the higher Consciousness making One of
Empathy, Love, Gratitude, Generosity, Truth, Caring
& Peace * Transmuting negative energies into Light ~
human kindness for All Life on the Planet*Om Shanti***:).

ABOUT SUNNY JETSUN

Inspired by the sixties Sunny started traveling the world in 1970. His spiritual journey on the hippie trail to India took him through San Francisco, Los Angeles, London, Amsterdam, Paris, Vancouver, Sidney, and Kathmandu to Varanasi. His arrival on the sub-continent was the beginning of writing autobiographical verses capturing his travel experiences, encounters with remarkable people and his quest for self-realization. Combining experimentation with drugs, sex, rock & roll, meditation, Love and life in general. Sunny started to open up to a multi-dimensional Universe. He lived the mantra, "Turn on, tune in, drop out" realising Mind's-illusions, inspired by deeper feelings of holistic nature, empathy, energy & Space ~

Over four decades Sunny has written and published 28 books of poetry, created over one hundred paintings, traveled the World and considers his masterpiece to be his daughter. He has spent the past fifteen years in Goa, India inspired by the freedom to experience and idealism of human consciousness.

Sunny Jetsun books and art are available on the web at:

Website: www.sunnyjetsun.com
Facebook: www.facebook.com/sunnyjetsun
Amazon: www.amazon.com/author/sunnyjetsun
Smashwords: www.smashwords.com/profile/view/sunnyjetsun

www.ingramcontent.com/pod-product-compliance
Lightning Source LLC
Chambersburg PA
CBHW020505030426
42337CB00011B/245